Elvis Presley

" I Want to Entertain People "

John Micklos, Jr.

Enslow Publishers, Inc.
40 Industrial Road
Box 398
Berkeley Heights, NJ 07922
USA

http://www.enslow.com

Library of Congress Cataloging-in-Publication Data

Micklos, John.
  Elvis Presley : "I want to entertain people" / John Micklos, Jr.
      p. cm. — (American rebels)
  Includes bibliographical references and index.
  Summary: "A biography of rock and roll legend Elvis Presley, discussing his early struggles with poverty, rise to fame as a controversial performer, personal hardships, and legacy"—Provided by publisher.
  ISBN 978-0-7660-3382-5
  1. Presley, Elvis, 1935-1977—Juvenile literature. 2. Rock musicians—United States—Biography—Juvenile literature. I. Title.
  ML3930.P73M53 2010
  782.42166092—dc22
  [B]
                                    2009017595

Printed in the United States of America

052010 Lake Book Manufacturing, Inc., Melrose Park, IL

10 9 8 7 6 5 4 3 2 1

To Our Readers: This book has not been authorized by Elvis Presley's estate or its successors. We have done our best to make sure all Internet Addresses in this book were active and appropriate when we went to press. However, the author and the publisher have no control over and assume no liability for the material available on those Internet sites or on other Web sites they may link to. Any comments or suggestions can be sent by e-mail to comments@enslow.com or to the address on the back cover.
Every effort has been made to locate all copyright holders of material used in this book. If any errors or omissions have occurred, corrections will be made in future editions of this book.

♻ Enslow Publishers, Inc., is committed to printing our books on recycled paper. The paper in every book contains 10% to 30% post-consumer waste (PCW). The cover board on the outside of each book contains 100% PCW. Our goal is to do our part to help young people and the environment too!

Illustration Credits: © Alain Le Garsmeur/Alamy, p. 128; Associated Press, pp. 7, 30, 38, 43, 48, 103, 135; Everett Collection, pp. 22, 64, 78, 86, 95, 105, 111; Lucas Jackson/Reuters/Landov, p. 132; National Archives and Records Administration, p. 113; Newhouse News Service/Landov, p. 70; © Pictorial Press Ltd/Alamy, p. 17; Regan Gealy Ozbirn, p. 12; Robert Williams/The Commercial Appeal/Landov, p. 74; Rue des Archives/The Granger Collection, New York, p. 59.

Cover Illustration: Everett Collection.

Contents

Chapter 1

Elvis Presley, the King

Screams erupted from the audience as Elvis Presley strode onstage in a plaid jacket to perform for *The Ed Sullivan Show* on September 9, 1956. The audience screamed again as he strummed his guitar and launched into his hit song "Don't Be Cruel." He followed that upbeat song with the mellow "Love Me Tender." Later in the program, Elvis performed "Ready Teddy" and two verses of "Hound Dog." Although his performance was relatively subdued, every movement "evoked screams" from the crowd.[1]

His performance also generated great interest among television viewers across the United States. A record audience of some 60 million people watched Elvis on *The Ed Sullivan Show* that night.[2]

What made this accomplishment even more amazing was the fact that Ed Sullivan had previously declared he would never invite Elvis on his show. Sullivan showcased many of the top talents of the time. An appearance on his show could help launch a career. He was determined

5

not to help Elvis build his fan base. Like many adults, Sullivan did not approve of Elvis's hip swinging and rock-and-roll singing. "He is not my cup of tea," Sullivan was quoted as saying.[3]

In fact, many adults believed that rock and roll represented a threat to authority. They viewed those who performed rock and roll as rebels. A singer such as Elvis who moved his body in such a provocative manner was even worse.

As it turned out, Elvis did not need Sullivan's help. During 1956 the Elvis phenomenon grew to massive proportions. Elvis had four number-one hits that year: "Heartbreak Hotel"; "I Want You, I Need You, I Love You"; "Don't Be Cruel/Hound Dog"; and "Love Me Tender." Together, those songs spent twenty-five weeks atop the music charts—nearly half the year.

"Heartbreak Hotel" opened the floodgates. On April 21, the song reached number one on *Billboard Magazine*'s chart of hot music hits. It remained at the top for eight weeks. "It marked Elvis's transition from a local southern sensation to a national phenomenon, and it built on the foundation begun by Bill Haley's '(We're Gonna) Rock Around the Clock,' to establish rock and roll as a musical force that was simply not going to go away," *Billboard* later wrote. "The king of rock and roll had just ascended to his throne."[4]

Finally, Sullivan realized he could not stop Elvis from becoming a star. Grudgingly, he spoke to Elvis's manager, Colonel Tom Parker, about having Elvis appear on his show, not once but three times. Parker demanded—and got—Elvis a fee of fifty thousand dollars for the

On September 9, 1956, Elvis Presley performed on *The Ed Sullivan Show*.

appearances. That was a remarkable figure at the time, far more than any other act could command.[5]

Elvis appeared again on *The Ed Sullivan Show* on October 28. This time he performed "Don't Be Cruel," "Love Me," "Love Me Tender," and "Hound Dog." He teased the audience by telling them that his last number would be a sad song with beautiful lyrics. Then he launched into a rocking rendition of "Hound Dog," complete with his trademark wild hip swinging and slightly sneering smile. The audience screamed in appreciation.

Young listeners loved Elvis and the new form of music he represented. Girls swooned over his sexy looks. Boys started to wear their hair slicked back like Elvis. Many parents and critics were less thrilled. Some were offended by the sensuality of Elvis. They thought it set a bad example for young men. They feared the way it excited young women. His wild performances earned him the nickname "Elvis the Pelvis," which Elvis found offensive.[6]

Critic Jack Gould of *The New York Times* put it this way: "When Presley executes his bumps and grinds, it must be remembered by the Columbia Broadcasting System that even the twelve-year-old's curiosity may be over-stimulated." Elvis's performance, Gould added, made a point for "the need for early sex education."[7]

Young listeners loved Elvis and the new form of music he represented.

Concern continued to mount. Indeed, on his third appearance on *The Ed Sullivan Show*, on January 6, 1957, he was filmed only from the waist up. That way, his swinging hips wouldn't offend anyone.[8]

Not all parents found Elvis objectionable, however. Indeed, some television historians believe Elvis's appearances on *The Ed Sullivan Show* helped "bridge the generation gap for Elvis's acceptance into the mainstream."[9]

Indeed, in the end Sullivan himself proclaimed Elvis "safe." Introducing Elvis's final number, Sullivan said, "This is a real decent, fine boy. We've never had a pleasanter experience on our show with a big name than we've had with you."[10]

Meanwhile, Elvis was conquering the world of film as well. In 1956 he went to Hollywood to film *Love Me Tender*. This Western drama was set just after the Civil War. It marked the only one of Elvis's films in which he did not receive top billing. Critics panned the film, but audiences loved it. It cemented Elvis's status as the most popular celebrity in America.

As 1957 began, Elvis Presley had truly earned his nickname of "the King." Hardly a passing fancy, as some believed he would be, he would reign as an icon of popular culture for two decades. Indeed, he became the first celebrity to be known by a single name—Elvis.

Over the years, Elvis's career evolved from rock-and-roll rebel to movie star to soldier to ballad crooner to Las Vegas performer. His body evolved from svelte to bloated. Through it all, he retained legions of fans who bought his records, watched his movies, and attended his stage shows. His meteoric rise to stardom was made all the more remarkable by his truly humble beginnings.

Chapter 2

The Twin Who Lived

Like much of Elvis Presley's early life, the circumstances surrounding his birth have become the subject of debate and legend over the years. But we do know the following facts. Around 4:00 A.M. on the frosty morning of January 8, 1935, Gladys Presley gave birth in her two-room house in Tupelo, Mississippi. The baby, named Jesse Garon, was born dead. Half an hour later, at 4:35 A.M., a second baby arrived. His name was Elvis Aaron.

Local legend says that the attending doctor, William Hunt, did not realize that Gladys had a second baby within her. She had to convince him that her labor pains were continuing. Years later, Elvis's younger cousin Billy Smith, said, "Dr. Hunt had no idea it was twins, although Gladys knew because she'd picked out the rhyming names."[1]

In truth, however, Dr. Hunt was an experienced physician. It seems likely that he would have known right away that a second baby was coming, especially since Gladys had thought for months that she was having twins. Still, the story about the "unexpected twin" became part of the folklore about Elvis.

Even the spelling of Elvis's middle name is a subject of debate. On the birth certificate it is listed as "Aron." Years later, Gladys said, "We matched their names. Jesse Garon and Elvis Aron."[2] Years later, Elvis changed the spelling of his middle to the more conventional "Aaron."

Gladys and Elvis spent time in the Tupelo hospital after his birth. Both needed further care after the ordeal of birth. Still, Gladys believed that "when one twin died, the one that lived got all the strength of both."[3]

She passed that belief on to Elvis. He remained fascinated with his twin throughout his life. Indeed, childhood friend James Ausborn recalled that Elvis would often take him to see Jesse's grave. There, he would "talk a little to Jesse and after the visit he was always lifted in his spirits."[4]

Living in Hard Times

In 1935, the United States was in the midst of the Great Depression. At the worst point, in 1933, one out of every four workers was unemployed. Among people not working on farms, the rate was even worse. More than one of three lacked a job.[5]

Like many other families, the Presleys were poor. In fact, Elvis's father, Vernon, could not pay the doctor's fifteen-dollar delivery fee after Elvis was born. In the end, welfare covered it.[6]

Vernon worked at a variety of odd jobs in Tupelo. At times, he was a milkman, sharecropper (a person who worked on an owner's farm for wages), a carpenter, and

The Tupelo, Mississippi, birthplace of Elvis Presley as it looks today.

a general laborer. A chronic bad back limited his ability to do some jobs. Beyond that, however, he also seemed to lack any ambition or drive.

Despite his faults, however, Vernon was very handsome. At the age of seventeen, he met twenty-one-year-old Gladys Love Smith. While Vernon was quiet, Gladys was lively. She loved dancing and music. She had moved to Tupelo from nearby West Point in the spring of 1933 after her father died.

Gladys ran a sewing machine in a garment factory that made men's shirts. She earned two dollars a day for a twelve-hour workday. Vernon and Gladys met at the First Assembly of God Tabernacle. They immediately fell in love. Within two months they eloped. They were totally unprepared for marriage. They had three major problems. First, they lacked the three-dollar fee for the license. Second, Vernon was not of legal age. Lastly, they had no place to live.[7]

The two young lovers did not let those details stop them. They managed to borrow the money for the license. Then, on Saturday, June 17, 1933, they traveled to a nearby county where no one knew them. Vernon claimed he was twenty-two, and Gladys said she was nineteen. She continued to shave years off her age for the rest of her life.

Gladys had lived a hard life. Her father died when she was nineteen. She provided much of the support for the family. She knew life would not get much easier when she married Vernon. She realized he was unlikely to have a successful career. "She simply accepted him for what he was: a ravishingly handsome, tenderhearted, unambitious young loafer," wrote Elvis biographer Elaine Dundy. "She loved him passionately and, without question, he returned her love."[8]

Perhaps because she had lost her other baby and because Elvis had been so fragile at birth, Gladys felt very protective of him. "She doted on him constantly," recalled longtime friend Lamar Fike, "a smothering kind of affection."[9]

When Elvis was just one year old, a tornado ripped through Tupelo. It killed more than two hundred people and injured more than three hundred others. The twister leveled much of the city. In fact, the storm destroyed the church across the road from the Presley family home but left their house untouched. The church was not rebuilt for several years. It served as a constant reminder to the Presley family of how lucky they were to be alive.

Elvis loved music all his life. At the age of two he climbed up the platform at church to sing with the members of the choir. He did not know the words of the hymns, but he still tried to sing along.

Everyone noticed how close Elvis was to his mother. The bond with his father was much less strong. Vernon was not nearly as loving as Gladys. He also drank too much sometimes. Often, he and Gladys argued.

In late 1937, life grew even harder for the Presley family after Vernon was arrested. He had been doing some work for a man named Orville Bean. At some point, he sold a hog to Bean. As the story went, Bean gave him a check for four dollars. No one knows what the arrangement was between the men, but Vernon decided that the fee for the hog was unfair. He and two other men changed the amount on the check. For his role in the crime, Vernon was sentenced to three years in prison.[10]

> **At the age of two he climbed up the platform at church to sing with the members of the choir.**

In the end, Vernon spent eight months at the Mississippi State Prison, then known as Parchman Farm. He was freed early on what was called a "hardship case." This meant that his family would have trouble getting by without him. That was certainly true in this case.

Gladys suffered greatly during Vernon's time in prison. She struggled just to keep food on the table for

14

her and young Elvis. Finally, she even had to give up the family's tiny home. She and Elvis moved in with relatives. Friends and neighbors also believed that she often drank during this period. She often appeared to have bloodshot eyes and the lingering aroma of alcohol.

Close to His Mother

During Vernon's absence, Gladys and Elvis grew even closer. Gladys doted on her young son. She took him to church. She even shared her bed with him. Elvis later recalled, "I was an only child—a very protected and spoiled only child."[11]

Based on the food available, Gladys tried to make Elvis's favorite meals. One food young Elvis loved was "soaks." This was corn bread dunked in buttermilk. He continued to enjoy "soaks" throughout his life. Other favorite foods included peanut butter and crackers; he also loved bananas.[12]

While Vernon was in prison, Elvis assumed the role of man of the house, although he was only three years old. He tried to comfort his mother when she felt sad. He patted her head and said, "There, there, my little baby."[13]

Elvis and his mother even developed their own secret language. They used it throughout their life. In fact, Fike, a member of Elvis's entourage, noted that you could be in a room with Elvis and Gladys "and not understand a word they were saying."[14]

They also had pet names for each other. Elvis's included "Ageless", "Naughty", and "Baby". Meanwhile, Elvis called Gladys "Satnin"—the brand name of a lard

15

product. That meant his mama was "chubby, round, and comfortable."[15]

Life did not improve much for the Presley family after Vernon came home. He felt that he had served his time and deserved a fresh start. He had more trouble than ever holding a job, however. Some people regarded him as a "jailbird."

Elvis and Gladys welcomed Vernon back. However, the relationships were strained. Throughout his growing up years, Elvis remained shy and restrained around his father. Meanwhile, Vernon and Gladys grew further and further apart. The one thing that held them together was Elvis.

Soon after Vernon returned, all three Presleys began having trouble sleeping, recalls Gladys's cousin Leona. Elvis began sleepwalking. He continued sleepwalking for a number of years, and he continued having trouble sleeping throughout his entire life.[16]

Finally, Vernon decided to seek a better life elsewhere. In 1940, the family moved to the port city of Pascagoula. Vernon had found a job in the shipyard there. They stayed only a few months before deciding to return to Tupelo. They moved around from one small rented place to another.

School Days

In September 1941 Elvis started first grade. Then in December 1941 the United States entered World War II following the Japanese attack on the U.S. naval base at Pearl Harbor, Hawaii.

Teachers recall Elvis as being quiet and shy. An average student, he did not attract a lot of attention from either teachers or classmates. Sometimes, however, other children taunted Elvis because his father had been in prison and often did not have a job. They even teased him for being poor. This was ironic since most of the families in East Tupelo were poor. The Presleys, however, were even poorer than most of their neighbors.

Elvis's third-grade class picture shows him standing apart from the other children. His arms were folded, and his hair was neatly combed. He

A young Elvis stands with his parents outside their Tupelo home in 1942.

had that familiar pouting smile for which he would later become famous. But, in the picture he seems disconnected from his peers.[17]

Throughout Elvis's youth, Gladys continued to shelter and protect Elvis. One time, a group of boys ganged up on Elvis as he walked home from school. Gladys jumped from the front porch. She chased the boys away with her broom.[18]

Once Elvis learned to read, he and friend Wayne Earnest often swapped comic books. That allowed them to double the number of comics they could afford to buy.

Like many other young boys, Elvis left his hard life behind as he lost himself in the adventures of the Lone Ranger, Tarzan, Batman, and Superman. His favorite superhero, though, was a new character named Captain Marvel, Jr. The young hero performed amazing feats. He even looked a lot like Elvis.[19]

By 1942, the United States was fully involved in World War II. Vernon went to northern Mississippi to help build a prisoner of war camp. It would house enemy soldiers captured during the fighting in Europe.

The following year Vernon moved to Memphis, Tennessee. There he worked in a factory that made munitions for the war effort. He stayed there throughout the war. He returned to Tupelo only on weekends.

Vernon thought about bringing his family to join him, but that did not work out. "I'd tramp all over town looking for so much as a single room," Vernon later recalled. "I'd find one, and first thing they would ask is, 'You got any children?' And I'd say I had a little boy. Then they'd shut . . . the door."[20]

While Vernon was gone, Gladys and Elvis kept on with their lives. Meanwhile, in addition to reading comics and playing childhood games, young Elvis began to more seriously pursue his real passion: music.

Chapter 3

Making Music

Elvis Presley was six years old when the first local radio station, WELO, was built in Tupelo. Charlie Boren served as its first announcer. On Saturday afternoons, WELO broadcast "Saturday Jamboree." This amateur program ran from 1:00 until 4:30 and featured local talent. Boren recalls that Elvis came every Saturday from the time he was about eight years old.

People got to sing or play simply by asking. "It was first come first served, and it was a big thing, those kids standing in line waiting for their chance, so if you were smart you got there early," Boren later recalled.[1]

Elvis soon became a regular performer. He sang a wide range of songs, ranging from cowboy tunes to gospel. One favorite was "Old Shep," a heart-wrenching ballad about a boy and his dog.

Over time, Elvis also struck up a friendship with a local musician named Carvel Lee Ausborn, who went by the stage name of Mississippi Slim. Slim toured across the United States playing country music. He never grew famous, but he played with many of the big names of the time. He even played at the Grand Ole Opry once or twice. Located in Nashville, Tennessee, the Grand Ole Opry is probably the world's most famous venue for country music. Almost all country music singers and musicians aspire to perform there.

Slim had a noontime show on Saturdays on WELO, just before "Saturday Jamboree." He also appeared on the Jamboree. Slim's younger brother James went to school with Elvis. "He was crazy about music," James recalled. "That's all he talked about." The boys would walk into town on Saturday, and Elvis would ask Slim to show him some chords. "I think gospel sort of inspired him [Elvis] to be in music," James said, "but then my brother helped carry it on."[2]

A Love of Gospel

Most of all, Elvis loved the kind of gospel music he heard in church. Even as a two-year-old, he had run down the aisle to join the choir, and he continued to enjoy that kind of music throughout his life.

One common legend through the years has been that Elvis and his parents formed a popular gospel trio that sang in local churches. Some people claimed that the talent he showed then foreshadowed his later success.

It makes a nice story, but the facts suggest it simply isn't true. While the Presley family almost certainly sang in church and may have sung together at home, there is no evidence to suggest that they sang as a traveling trio. Elvis himself later recalled that "I sang some with my folks in the Assembly of God church choir [but] it was a small church, so you couldn't sing too loud." He told another reporter that he "trioed" with his parents, but only in church.[3]

On many other occasions, he spoke about the role of church music in his development as a singer. Years later, when criticized for his wild gyrations while performing, Elvis said the habit dated back to watching gospel singers in church. "They're not afraid to move their bodies, and that's where I got it," he said. "When I started singing, I just did what came natural, what they taught me. God is natural."[4]

Talent Show Winner

At the age of ten, Elvis sang in a talent show at the annual Mississippi-Alabama Fair and Dairy Show at the fairgrounds in the middle of downtown Tupelo. As the story goes, his fifth-grade teacher was impressed by his singing. She took him to the principal, who then entered him in the radio talent contest sponsored by WELO on Children's Day (October 3, 1945) at the fair.

> "When I started singing, I just did what came natural, what they taught me. God is natural."

The five-day fair marked an annual highlight in Tupelo. That year, performers from the Grand Ole Opry Company were slated to appear, including Minnie Pearl. Elvis later recalled his performance in the children's competition. "I wore glasses, no music, and I won, I think it was fifth place in this state talent contest," he said. He also recalled getting a whipping from Gladys Presley that day—possibly for going on a ride she considered too dangerous.[5]

21

Elvis Presley in his early teens.

Gladys recalled the event, too—without the whipping. "Elvis had no way to make music, and the other kids wouldn't accompany him. He just climbed up on a chair so he could reach the microphone and he sang 'Old Shep.'"[6]

Years later, Elvis recalled the event, saying, "I just went out there and started singing. I'd set my heart on singing and nothing in the world could have stopped me from entering the talent contest. I did it all on my own."[7]

Moving Around

Meanwhile, other things were happening that seemed to signal an upward turn in the fortunes of the Presley family. World War II ended in the summer of 1945. That brought an end to Vernon Presley's job in the war plant in Memphis. It meant he could come home to Tupelo to be with his family.

During the war, the Presleys had managed to save a bit of money. On August 18, 1945, they bought a brand-new, four-room house on Berry Street in Tupelo. The purchase price of two thousand dollars seemed high for the time, but there was a housing shortage after the war as millions of servicemen and servicewomen returned home. The Presleys paid two hundred dollars in cash as a down payment. They had to make monthly payments of thirty dollars plus 6 percent interest. Ironically, the Presleys bought this house from Orville Bean. This was the same man who had Vernon put in prison years earlier for altering his check.

Vernon hoped that owning a house would raise the family's status in the community. He took a further step to improving his reputation when he became a deacon in the First Assembly of God Church.

Within a year, however, the family moved again, this time to a house in town. They could no longer afford the payment on the house on Berry Street. First they moved to a small rented house on Commerce Street. Next they moved to a house on Mulberry Alley near where Vernon worked.

In moving to the main part of town, the Presley family once again became the object of scorn. In East Tupelo, they had at least fit in to some extent with the other working-class families. In Tupelo, they were once again the poorest of the poor.

First Guitar

Accounts vary about when Elvis got his first guitar. Some say he received it as a gift for his ninth or tenth birthday. However, another account says he got it the day after a major storm that frightened Gladys and him. A small tornado hit Tupelo on January 7, 1946, the day before Elvis's eleventh birthday, so that makes January 8, 1946, the most likely date.

Regardless of when Elvis got his guitar, we know it was purchased at a hardware store run by F. L. Bobo. Bobo recalled that when Elvis and his mother came in that day Elvis wanted to buy a rifle. Elvis had saved up his money, but he did not have enough to buy the rifle. Gladys wanted him to buy a guitar instead. According to Bobo, she told Elvis that she would make up the difference for him to buy a guitar, but not a rifle.[8]

According to another account, Elvis wanted a bicycle instead of the guitar. Again, Gladys tried to help Elvis make his decision. "Son, wouldn't you rather have the guitar?" Gladys said. "It would help you with your singing, and everyone does enjoy hearing you sing."[9]

In the end, Elvis made a fateful decision. He decided to get the guitar. According to legend, the guitar cost $12.00. Bobo said the cost was actually $7.75.[10]

Several people helped Elvis learn to play his new instrument. His Uncle Vester, who sometimes performed in honky-tonks and at country dances, taught him a few chords. So did his Uncle Johnny. But it was the new pastor, twenty-one-year-old Frank Smith, who really helped Elvis learn to play.

Smith recalled that Elvis bought a book that showed where to place your fingers. "I went over to his house a time or two, or he would come to where I was, and I would show him some runs and different chords from what he was learning out of his books," Smith said. "That was all: not enough to say I taught him how to play, but I helped him."[11]

As his skill and confidence grew, Elvis began playing at the special singing portion of the church service. At first, he was shy. Smith had to call on him to perform. "I would have to insist on him [getting up there], he didn't push himself," Smith recalled. "He sang quite a few times, and he was liked."[12]

Meanwhile, Elvis also was expanding his music horizons. He began to teach himself to play the piano. He had many chances to use the pianos at his church and his school. Whereas he struggled to learn the guitar, he found that he had a natural gift for playing the piano. He learned quickly and soon felt that the piano was his best instrument. In fact, throughout his career, he never rated himself very highly as a guitarist.

In the fall of 1946, Elvis started sixth grade in a new school called Milam. Again, he seemed to hang quietly around the edges, trying to fit in. In his sixth-grade class picture, he is the only child in overalls. Later, when Elvis became wealthy, he never wore overalls or even denim jeans. In fact, he did not even want anyone around him to wear denim. It reminded him of the poverty he had left behind.[13]

By the time Elvis entered seventh grade, the Presleys were living in a rented house on North Green Street. The house was nice, but it was in a neighborhood of mostly black families. In the 1940s there were few integrated neighborhoods in most southern towns. Black families and white families generally lived in different areas. In fact, some of the Presleys' old friends refused to visit them in their new home because they did not want to go into that part of town.[14]

In seventh grade, Elvis began taking his guitar to school almost every day. Often he would play and sing in the school basement, which served as a recess area. "He brought his guitar to school when it wasn't raining," his friend James Ausborn later recalled. "He'd bring his guitar swung over his back and put it in his locker till lunchtime. Then everybody would set around, and he

In seventh grade, Elvis began taking his guitar to school almost every day. would sing and strum on that guitar. All he talked about was music—not the Opry so much as gospel music. That was what he sung mostly."[15]

The guitar did not make Elvis particularly popular, however. Most of his classmates described him as shy or a loner. Others made fun of him for playing "hillbilly" music. Still, Elvis often sang during the weekly homeroom activity time. Furthermore, he often told classmates that someday he would sing at the Grand Ole Opry.[16]

Young Elvis had a second love besides singing—girls. He constantly flirted with the girls at his school. Few showed any interest in him. Indeed, "anyone wishing to provoke a little girl to tears of rage had only to chalk 'Elvis loves—' and then write the girl's name on the blackboard when the teacher was out of the room," wrote Elvis biographer Elaine Dundy.[17]

Near the beginning of his eighth-grade year, a group of tough boys cut the strings on Elvis's guitar. Some of the other boys in his class pooled their money and bought him another set. Then, suddenly, Elvis was gone. The first week of November in 1948 he announced that he was moving to Memphis, Tennessee. Vernon had decided to try to establish a new life in a new city.

On his last day of school, Elvis gave a little concert for his classmates. The last song he sang was "A Leaf on a Tree." Classmate Leroy Green later claimed that he went up to Elvis at the end and said, "Elvis, one of these days you're gonna be famous." Little did he know just how prophetic those words would be.[18]

Chapter 4

Moving to Memphis

In November 1948, the Presley family headed off to Memphis, Tennessee, in search of a better life. Elvis Presley later recalled, "Dad packed all our belongings in boxes and put them on the top and in the trunk of a 1939 Plymouth."[1]

They were joined on their journey by the family of Gladys Presley's brother, Travis Smith. There were seven riders in the car, as well as all of both families' belongings. It was a long and hard ride. Elvis's cousin Billy Smith later summed it up this way: "I was five years old, but I remember every dang mile."[2]

At first the move to Memphis did not seem to greatly improve any of their lives. At first all seven of them lived in a house, sharing a single bathroom. Then Gladys found work as a sewing machine operator at Fashion Curtains. Later Vernon Presley got a job at Precision Tool Company. Eventually, the Presleys moved out. But they still had little space and even less privacy. "The places that they moved in up there didn't seem

much better than what they had down here," said
Gladys's cousin Corinne Richards Tate.[3]

Nonetheless, Gladys worked to convince her relatives
to move north to join them. Eventually, most of the
family moved to Memphis.

In June 1949, the Presley family applied to move
into public housing. Vernon now had a job as a loader at
United Paint, earning about forty dollars a week with
overtime. Jane Richardson of the Memphis Housing
Authority interviewed Gladys and Elvis. In her notes,
Richardson wrote: "Cook, eat and sleep in one room.
Share bath. No privacy . . . Need Housing. Persons
interviewed are Mrs. Presley and son. Nice boy. They
seem very nice and deserving."[4]

High School Years

The Presleys moved into the Lauderdale Courts public
housing project in September 1949, just as Elvis was
beginning his freshman year at Humes High School. At
the time, the Courts housed many families like the
Presleys. These were hardworking but low-income
families who were trying to make their way in the world
and hoping for better lives for their children.

To the Presleys, the apartment marked a huge step
forward in their standard of living. They went from
living in a single room to having two bedrooms, a living
room, a kitchen, and a bathroom they did not have to
share with another family.

Both Gladys and Vernon wanted Elvis to have a full
high-school education. In those days, many working-class
children dropped out when they were fifteen or sixteen to

get full-time jobs. The Presleys, however, believed a high-school diploma was the key to a better life.

Indeed, Vernon recalled walking with Elvis on his first day in his new school. Then Vernon returned home. Soon after, Elvis came back, too. He found the huge school overwhelming. He was "so nervous he was bug-eyed," Vernon said.[5]

During his first two years at Humes High, Elvis melted into the crowd. He was an average student, earning mostly average grades—Bs in many subjects with a smattering of As. In eighth grade, he earned one interesting C—in music. He claimed that the teacher, Miss Marmann, simply did not appreciate his type of singing.[6]

Teachers found him shy and polite. "He was a gentle, obedient boy, and he always went out of his way to try to do what you asked him to do," said Susie Johnson, his ninth-grade homeroom teacher. "He was during his first years in our school a shy boy," added Mildred Scrivener, his twelfth-grade homeroom and history teacher.[7]

Over time, Elvis began to feel more at home in Memphis. He made friends with Buzzy Forbess, Paul Dougher, and Farley Guy in his building. Together the four boys played football, rode bikes, and hung out at the local public pool during warm weather. They wandered through the downtown section of town. Sometimes they even ventured onto Beale Street, which was home to many well-known clubs featuring blues music.

Creating His Own Style

Just as Elvis found himself drawn to that style of music, he found himself drawn to a new style of clothing as well.

Elvis's high-school
yearbook photo

He bought some of these clothes used in thrift shops. Other items came from Lansky Brothers, a clothing store that catered to musicians.

One day Elvis was standing outside Lansky's store looking through the window at the clothes inside. The owner, Bernard Lansky, invited him to come in and look around. At the end of his visit, Elvis said, "Mr. Lansky, when I'm rich, I'm gonna buy you out." "Don't buy me out," Lansky responded. "Buy from me." And Elvis did. He became a regular customer for the next twenty years.[8]

At a time when most kids dressed in jeans and simple shirts, Elvis often wore black pants and pink shirts. He let his hair grow long and groomed it with hair tonic and Vaseline until it was slick and stiff. He grew sideburns as well. He certainly stood out in the crowd.

On more than one occasion, Elvis's hair caused problems at school. One year, he decided to try out for the football team. The coach took one look at Elvis and told him that he would have to cut his hair first. In the end, Elvis decided it wasn't worth it.

Another time, a bunch of guys cornered Elvis and threatened to cut his hair. A boy named Bobby "Red" West stepped in to stop them. Red was a big kid—a football player. The other kids backed down. Red became a lifelong friend to Elvis. In fact, once Elvis became famous, Red became a sometime bodyguard for many years.

Among Elvis's more interesting activities in high school was joining the Reserve Officers' Training Corps (ROTC). That might have seemed out of character for someone who dressed so wildly and wore his hair so long. Still, he enjoyed doing the precision drills and wearing the uniform. In fact, years later, he donated money so that the ROTC drill team at Humes could buy brand-new uniforms.

> **At a time when most kids dressed in jeans and simple shirts, Elvis often wore black pants and pink shirts.**

Going to Work

Throughout his high-school years, Elvis held a variety of part-time jobs. First he cut lawns using a push mower that Vernon bought him. Then he worked as an usher at Loew's State Theater in downtown Memphis. He gave some of the money to his parents to help make ends meet. The rest he kept for clothes, buying cheeseburgers and fries with friends after school, and dates.

Despite Elvis chipping in, the Presley family continued to struggle financially. Vernon continued to change jobs frequently. Chronic back problems prevented him from doing many of the manual labor jobs for which he was best suited. Gladys worked a variety of jobs, too, when the family needed money. The job she found most satisfying was working as a nurses' aide at nearby St. Joseph Hospital. Patients complimented her so often that the head nurse suggested that she consider doing the training to be a regular nurse. Finances and her lack of education made that impossible, however.

Moreover, Gladys suffered with her own health problems. Most of those problems revolved around drinking. For one thing, Gladys hated to see her precious little boy growing up. She also felt frustrated at the family's lack of financial security. Often, she and Vernon argued about money. To forget about her problems, she turned more and more often to alcohol. Sometimes she took diet pills as well. The combination took a toll on her health.

At one point when both Vernon and Gladys were unemployed, Elvis began working a full-shift job from 3:00 to 11:00 P.M. in addition to attending school. Soon, however, he began falling asleep in class, and his grades plummeted. The school counselor called in his parents and told them that Elvis needed to make a decision—school or work. In the end, he chose school.

At one point, the Presleys fell behind in their rent at Lauderdale Courts. They were threatened with eviction. For awhile they went on welfare, much to Gladys's shame. Then at another point when both Gladys and Vernon had relatively stable jobs, they earned too much to live in the projects. Finally, on January 7, 1953, just before Elvis's eighteenth birthday, they moved out of the projects forever. After a brief stay on Cypress Street, they ended up on Alabama Avenue, directly across from their old apartment. But at least this time they were on their own.

Dating

Meanwhile, Elvis maintained his interest in girls while in high school. His first real crush was on a girl named

Sue who worked at the candy counter of the movie theater where Elvis worked as an usher. She gave him free candy. He ended up getting fired for punching another usher who tattled on them.[9]

Elvis dated many girls in high school. "He liked to date," recalled his friend Buzzy Forbess. "He wasn't the sort to just walk up and ask for dates right off, though. And the girls he did go out with, they were pretty affectionate; they really cared for him."[10]

He went to the senior prom with Regis Wilson Vaughn, the girl he was dating at the time. Still, he had not been really serious about any of the girls he dated throughout high school.

Honing His Musical Skill

Although Elvis did not carry his guitar to school every day in Memphis as he had done in Tupelo, he maintained his interest in music throughout high school. Memphis was home to blues legend B. B. King and many other blues artists. You could also find many other styles of music there, including hillbilly and gospel.

Jesse Lee Denson, the son of a preacher, gave Elvis guitar lessons. Together with some other boys, they gave informal concerts on Market Mall, a path that ran through the middle of the Courts apartments. At night, Elvis practiced alone.

Elvis also became a regular at a little record store called Charlie's. Lots of teenagers hung out there to listen to songs on the jukebox. One time Elvis told Johnny Black, another musician who spent time at Charlie's, "Johnny, someday I'm going to be driving

Cadillacs." It was a sign that even then he aspired to greatness.[11]

At noon on Saturdays—and sometimes during the week if he cut school—Elvis would go downtown to the WMPS radio studio for the *High Noon Round-Up* show. The Blackwood Brothers Quartet appeared live there. The group was known nationally for its country and gospel singing. Formed in 1934, the group continued to perform into the twenty-first century.

James Blackwood, one of the group's founders, remembered Elvis from those days. So did Jack Hess, lead singer for the Statesmen, another gospel group. What made Elvis stand out from the hundreds of other fans? "We didn't know Elvis Presley from a sack of sand," Hess said. "He was just nice, a nice kid, this bright-eyed boy asking all kinds of questions, and asking in a way that you would really want to tell him. . . . He wanted to know if he would be handicapped because he couldn't read music."[12]

Elvis also became a regular at the All-Night Gospel Singings. They had started at Ellis Auditorium in Memphis and spread throughout the South. At the age of eighteen, he even auditioned for the Songfellows Quartet, but he was turned down.

Toward the end of his senior year in high school, Elvis participated in the senior class variety show. Approximately thirty acts took part. The performer who received the most applause would be the winner of the competition. Elvis won easily. Then he performed an encore that received even louder applause. Observers said that many in the audience cried during his performance. It is said that one girl even fainted. Elvis went offstage and told Miss Scrivener, the teacher who served as the show's producer, "They really liked me, Miss Scrivener. They really liked me."[13]

On June 3, 1953, Elvis received his diploma from Humes High School. He took great pride in this accomplishment. Indeed, he became the first member of his immediate family to earn a diploma. He displayed it proudly for many years.

According to his senior yearbook, Elvis had participated fully in the high-school experience. It listed his major as Shop, History, and English. His activities included ROTC, News Club, History Club, and Speech. He was not voted most popular or most talented in his class. The graduate who would later become one of the most world's most famous people drew very little notice among his classmates.

> **"They really liked me, Miss Scrivener. They really liked me."**

Still, the Humes High senior class prophecy included a mention of Elvis that hinted at things to come. It said, "We are reminded at this time to not forget to invite you all out to the 'Silver Horse' on Onion [sic] Ave. to hear the singing hillbillies of the road. Elvis Presley, Albert Teague, Doris Wilburn, and Mary Ann Propst are doing a bit of picking and singing out that-away."[14]

Chapter 5

Breaking Through

After high school, Elvis Presley took the first decent- paying job offered. He worked briefly at Parker Machinists Shop. After a few months he took a job at Precision Tool Company. He hated the work, but he was proud of being able to help support the family.

In January 1954 Elvis found a job that suited him better. He became a truck driver for Crown Electric. He enjoyed being outside rather than stuck inside a factory. Even better, he earned forty-five dollars a week. That was good money in 1954. A gallon of milk cost ninety-two cents that year. A gallon of gas cost twenty-one cents, and a loaf of bread cost seventeen cents.[1]

Elvis gave most of the money he earned to his parents. He took out just enough to cover his expenses for the week. He carried his guitar with him in the truck many days. Mrs. Gladys Tipler, who owned the company with her husband, sometimes teased him about it. "Elvis, put down that gi-tar," she said. "It's gonna be the ruination of you. You better make up your mind what you're gonna do."[2]

Making His First Records

In many ways, he already had decided what he was going to do. Elvis used some of the money he earned over the summer of 1953 to go into the recording studio for the first time. He went to Memphis Recording Service, which later became known as Sun Studio. There he paid about four dollars to record "My Happiness" and "That's When Your Heartaches Begin." He gave the record to his mother as a present.

Elvis told office manager Marion Keisker that he liked to sing all kinds of music. Asked who he sounded like, he replied, "I don't sound like nobody." At the end of his session, Keisker made this note: "Good ballad singer. Hold."[3]

> He went to Memphis Recording Service, which later became known as Sun Studio.

Also, owner Sam Phillips had told her that he was searching for a white man who had the sound and feel of a black musician. Keisker thought she might have found the right person in Elvis.

Still, nothing came of that contact for some time. Elvis met Phillips when he returned to the studio in January 1954. This time he recorded two country songs, "I'll Never Stand in Your Way" and "It Wouldn't Be the Same Without You." Phillips still did not have any assignment for him, and Elvis began to wonder if he would ever get his "break." Keisker, however, believed

One of Elvis's first records was the song "I'll Never Stand in Your Way."

things would work out for the young singer. "He was so ingenious there was no way he could go wrong," she later said.[4]

Dating Dixie

In January 1954, nineteen-year-old Elvis began attending the Assembly of God Church in Memphis. The church had nearly two thousand members, including the famous Blackwood Brothers Quartet. The group often performed during church services.

It was through the church that Elvis first saw fourteen-year-old Dixie Locke, who found herself strangely attracted to the shy young man with the greasy black hair and colorful clothes. Soon after that she introduced herself to him at a Sunday evening event at the Rainbow Rollerdrome. The two immediately hit it off.

Elvis described Dixie this way: "She was kind of small with long, dark hair that came down to her shoulders and the biggest smile I've ever seen anywhere. She was always laughing, always enjoying herself. . . . I gave her my high school ring. . . . For two years we had a ball."[5]

For months, Elvis and Dixie spent nearly all their time together. Often they would go to Riverside Park, which was full of young couples. Many times, Elvis would get out his guitar and sing. "People were just mesmerized, and he loved being the center of attention," Dixie recalled. "I think he could have sung to everybody in the entire city of Memphis and not cared at all."[6]

In May 1954, Elvis auditioned to join Eddie Bond and his band, the Stompers. Elvis was crushed when Bond rejected him. He later claimed that Bond told him to "go back to driving a truck."[7]

Dixie and her family went on an extended trip for much of the summer. Both she and Elvis promised to remain faithful while she was away.

Breaking Through

Elvis spent much of the summer building his career. Phillips had finally given him a call. Phillips was looking for a singer to record a song titled "Without You." He couldn't even remember Elvis's name. He asked for the "kid with the sideburns." According to Keisker, when she called, Elvis literally ran all the way to the studio, arriving out of breath while she was still holding the phone.[8]

Elvis did not feel that he captured any magic with the song, and it was never released. However, Phillips was impressed enough to invite Elvis to continue singing. For the next couple of hours, he sang a little bit of everything—blues, gospel, and country.

Phillips believed that Elvis could succeed with the proper backing. Soon after, he brought Elvis into the studio to rehearse with talented bass player Bill Black and guitarist Scotty Moore. Moore later recalled, "He came to my house for like a pre-audition. I was very impressed. . . . It seemed like he knew every song in the world."[9]

Phillips told the three young men to rehearse until they got a style. On July 5, 1954, Elvis recorded "That's All Right," his version of a song recorded by noted blues artist Arthur Crudup in the 1940s. The ballads that Elvis recorded for Phillips did not take off, but everyone could sense the magic in this upbeat number, which seemed a cross between country music and blues music. It became Elvis's first hit.

On July 8, the song made its debut on the local "Red Hot and Blue" show on radio Station WHBQ. Elvis was so nervous about the song that he hid in a local theater that evening. There his parents found him and told him that the radio disc jockey wanted to interview him.

When Elvis arrived for his interview, he was so nervous that he shook all over. The interviewer asked where Elvis had gone to high school. "I wanted to get that out, because a lot of people listening had thought he was colored," the interviewer said. Like Phillips wanted, Elvis had captured the sound of an African-American singer.[10]

Due to the heavy volume of requests, the disc jockey played the record an amazing fourteen times in a row. In all, seven thousand people requested the song that night.

Records in those days had an "A" side (the hit) and a "B" side. Within a few days, Elvis recorded an old country song called "Blue Moon of Kentucky" to place on the flip side of "That's All Right." The two songs were officially released on July 19. Soon "That's All Right" rose to number three on the Memphis country-and-western chart.[11]

Later that month, Elvis signed a formal contract with Sun Records. Because he was under twenty-one years of age, his parents had to sign it as well. The two-year contract called for a minimum of eight record sides over a period of two years. The royalty rate was 3 percent of the wholesale price. In addition, Moore became manager for the new group.

Later in July, Elvis performed his first concert. He served as the opening act for well-known country singer Slim Whitman at the Overton Park Shell in Memphis. His parents and Dixie, who had returned from her summer trip, attended. Elvis later said that he was so nervous onstage that his legs began to shake. Thus began the leg shake that would become his trademark.[12]

Later in July, Elvis performed his first concert.

As Elvis sang that day, the crowd hooted. He thought they were making fun of him, and he slunk offstage after singing "Blue Moon of Kentucky."

41

But his friends backstage were elated. They realized the crowd's noises meant they were excited by the music. His friends pushed him back onstage for an encore. "The girls love you," they told him. "It's the way you shake."[13]

Momentum quickly built both for Elvis and his record. In early August, *Billboard* published a review in its "Spotlight" section. Editor Paul Ackerman called Elvis "A potent new chanter who can sock over a tune for either the country or the r & b [rhythm and blues] markets. . . . A strong new talent."[14] *Billboard* was a respected music magazine. Its endorsement helped set the stage for Elvis's popularity to move beyond Memphis.

His friend Red West from high school was amazed to hear the song on the radio. "It was bigger than life," he said. "I was happy for him, but it was kind of unbelievable."[15]

Soon things started happening in a blur. For a couple of months, Elvis juggled his work as a truck driver, his singing, and his relationship with Dixie. For Dixie, looking back, wrote Elvis biographer Peter Guralnick, "it was easy to say that this was the point at which it all began to end, this was the point at which she lost him and the world claimed him, but at the time she was just so proud of him."[16]

Offers to perform continued to pile up. Elvis, Scotty, and Bill began playing each weekend in the Eagle's Nest, a popular nightclub in Memphis. Then on October 2, they fulfilled a fantasy that every country musician dreams about. They got to play at the Grand Ole Opry in Nashville, Tennessee. The Grand Ole Opry is the most renowned place in country music. To be invited

In 1954, Elvis (far left) stands with his bandmates Bill Black and Scotty Moore. Sam Phillips is on the far right.

there was a great tribute to a singer and band that had been together just a few months and had just two songs to their credit.

According to some reports, Elvis earned polite, but unenthusiastic, applause. Others said the performance was a disaster. One popular story circulated over the years is that Jim Denny, the director of the Grand Ole Opry, told Elvis that he ought to stick to driving a truck. Other historians don't believe that ever happened. They report that Denny said Elvis was "not bad" but not right for the Grand Ole Opry. Coming from Denny, who was very critical, that was a positive comment. At least Phillips of Sun Records took it that way.[17]

Just about the same time, Elvis and his band released their second record. It was titled "Good Rockin' Tonight/I Don't Care If the Sun Don't Shine." The record became popular in Memphis but never really caught on elsewhere.

Meanwhile, however, Elvis, Scotty, and Bill landed a spot on the *Louisiana Hayride*, a weekly show in Shreveport, Louisiana, that helped launch the careers of many country stars. During their first performance, the audience did not quite know what to make of Elvis and his band. Most performers wore Western clothing. Elvis wore a sport coat. Furthermore, Elvis sounded different from anyone they had ever heard before. However, the teenagers in the audience soon were captivated by his look and his music.

Elvis and his band soon earned an invitation to play every Saturday night for a year. Every weekend the band made the seven-hour drive from Memphis to Shreveport to perform. Elvis was to receive eighteen dollars per show, while Scotty and Bill would earn twelve dollars apiece.

Around this time, Elvis quit his job as a truck driver and made a commitment to make his living as a singer. Plus, singing had become a full-time job. In addition to playing at the *Louisiana Hayride*, Elvis and his band traveled for performances in Texas and Arkansas.

Elvis soon became the most popular performer at the *Louisiana Hayride*. Fans adored him. Therefore, his act always closed the show. It was at his last performance ever at the *Louisiana Hayride* that the announcer stated, "Elvis has left the building" as a way to calm down the crowd. The announcer was afraid that the audience would try to intercept Elvis on his way out, as often happened at his shows. In the 1970s, "Elvis has left the building" became a fairly standard line for closing his shows.

In late December 1954, Elvis signed a management contract with Bob Neal, a disc jockey at WMPS in Memphis. In a Memphis newspaper article, Elvis was quoted as saying that increasing demands for appearances made a manager necessary.[18]

Before year's end, he released another record titled "Milkcow Blues Boogie/You're a Heartbreaker." He also bought a tan 1951 Lincoln for the group to do its traveling. On the side was painted the words: "Elvis Presley—Sun Records."[19]

> "Elvis has left the building" became a fairly standard line for closing his shows.

Elvis made some other purchases as well. He bought himself a 1942 Martin guitar. It cost him one hundred seventy-five dollars, which was a great deal of money in those days. The man at the store bought his used guitar for eight dollars and promptly threw it in the trash. To Elvis, this seemed like a waste. "Shucks, it still played good," he said.[20]

For Christmas, Elvis bought Dixie some fancy clothing that she really liked. They spent all Christmas Day together, but he had to leave immediately after for a performance December 28 in Houston.

In just a few short months, Elvis had gone from an unknown singer to a fast-rising star. But his success in 1954 was nothing compared to what lay ahead in 1955. Elvis mania would soon sweep the United States and beyond.

Chapter 6

Ascending the Throne

Elvis Presley had many reasons to be excited as 1955 began. He continued to tour. On January 5, he topped the bill at the City Auditorium in San Angelo, Texas, although they misspelled his name as "Alvis Presley." At the end of the show, hundreds of teenaged girls rushed the stage seeking autographs.[1] He continued on a whirlwind tour for the rest of January that carried him through stops in Texas, Arkansas, Louisiana, and Mississippi.

Under Bob Neal's guidance, and with Elvis's popularity steadily growing, the band kept busy. Elvis and Scotty Moore and Bill Black did three or four shows a week. Neal's wife, Helen, would "stand at the door with a cigar box and sell the tickets, and I'd get up and tell a few of my jokes, M.C. the show," Neal later recalled. "Usually we took in about three hundred dollars."[2]

It soon became clear that Elvis drew most of the fans to their shows. To this point, Elvis had been receiving 50 percent of the money. Neal proposed that instead of getting a percentage, Scotty and Bill should receive a salary. In the end, Elvis had to make the decision, and Neal had to pass it along to Scotty and Bill. Needless to say, they did not appreciate the change. In fact, frustration grew to the point that Scotty and Bill threatened to quit. In the end, however, they agreed to stay.

> **It soon became clear that Elvis drew most of the fans to their shows.**

Elvis's popularity soon grew to the point were he found himself in danger from fans of both genders. Girls loved him. They swooned at his hip-swinging performances. Meanwhile, their boyfriends boiled with jealousy. For a performance in Lubbock, Texas, Elvis had police protection all day. But after the deputies went home at the end of the evening, a man in a car called Elvis to come over. When Elvis did so, the man punched Elvis in the face and sped off.

The full effect Elvis had on girls can be seen in a show at the Gator Bowl football stadium in Florida in May 1955. During the show, he joked that he'd see the girls in the audience backstage after the show. A gate had been left open, and girls poured into the backstage area. They literally ripped most of the clothes off his body in their frenzy. He felt lucky to escape without getting seriously hurt.

Elvis Meets the Colonel

It was clear that Elvis was becoming a bigger and bigger star. But he was starting to get frustrated with playing the same clubs and recording the same types of songs. He wanted to break through on a national level. Then

Colonel Tom Parker (left) took over the management of Elvis's career in the 1950s.

he met a man who offered to help him do just that—Colonel Tom Parker.

Parker was not really a colonel, and Parker was not even really his name. His real name was Andreas Cornelius van Kuijk, and he had come to America from Holland in 1929. Once here, he changed his name.

Parker had a colorful background. For several years he worked in a carnival. He also claimed to have served in the U.S. Army, despite the fact that he was not even a U.S. citizen. Some people dispute that claim. In the 1940s he served as field director of the Tampa, Florida, Humane Society.

After that, Parker started managing performers. For a while, he managed country star Eddy Arnold. He helped

Arnold reach the top of the country charts. But the two got into an argument, and Arnold fired him.

Parker sought a new performer he could make into a star. When he heard about the following that twenty-year-old Elvis was building, he was intrigued. He began attending some of his concerts. He saw at once that the singer had a special magnetism. He realized that Elvis's popularity could generate the kind of riots that singer Frank Sinatra had inspired in the 1940s. "And from then on, when he went to Elvis's shows, it was the crowd Parker watched, not Elvis," wrote biographer Alanna Nash.[3]

In February 1955 Parker met with Sam Phillips and Neal to talk about Elvis's future. He told Phillips that Elvis could not succeed on a small-time label such as Sun. Parker said that he had already inquired at major label RCA about buying out the contract. Needless to say, Phillips was not happy at the thought of losing his biggest recording star. He rebuffed Parker's offer, but Parker began helping Neal expand Elvis's concert bookings into new areas.

Amid all the touring, Elvis, Scotty, and Bill took time to record some new songs. One of these songs, "Baby Let's Play House" became the next single. The song had been written and first recorded by blues singer Arthur Gunter, but Elvis injected his own personality into his version. He also changed some of the words, a habit he maintained throughout his recording career.

Amid all the success, Elvis did have one disappointment. He auditioned for *Arthur Godfrey's Talent Scouts* in New York. He hoped exposure on the popular television show could help take his music nationwide. He, the band, and Neal flew to New York, but the audition did not go well. They never even got to meet Godfrey. The lady conducting the interview had a "don't call us, we'll call you" attitude, which meant she wasn't very interested.[4]

Breaking Up

Still, Elvis and his band kept touring nearly nonstop throughout the spring and summer. On May 6, Elvis returned to Memphis to attend Dixie Locke's junior prom. Soon after, however, they broke up. The rigors of his touring life tore them apart. Sometimes while he was away, Dixie spent the night with his parents. But she was able to spend less and less time with him.

Indeed both Dixie and Gladys Presley sensed that the man they both loved was slipping away from them. "I think she really had trouble accepting him as his popularity grew," Dixie said. "It grew hard for her to let everybody have him. I had the same feelings. He did not belong to [us] anymore."[5]

In the end, Elvis accused Dixie of dating other people when he was on the road. Actually, it was the other way around. He often slept with some of the women who flocked to see his shows. By September 1955, their relationship had ended. Dixie told Gladys that she planned to marry another man. She asked Gladys to tell Elvis. She couldn't bear to do it herself, she said.

Making the Charts

The summer of 1955 flew by in a blur, with several adventures along the way. On June 5, while traveling

50

through Arkansas, Elvis's pink-and-white Cadillac caught fire and burned. Bill was driving when the wheel bearing went out. "All of a sudden he realized the damn thing was on fire," recalled Scotty, who was in a separate car ahead of Bill. "He couldn't put it out. All he could do was open the trunk and throw our clothes and instruments out all over the road."[6]

In July 1955, "Baby, Let's Play House" became Elvis's first record to make the nationwide country music charts. These charts reflect the popularity of songs across America. Also that month, both Elvis and Scotty bought new guitars. Elvis got a Martin D-28. It came with a tooled leather cover that prevented the back of the instrument from getting scratched by Elvis's belt buckle when he performed.

Elvis and the band took some time off from the road in July to record three new songs. Those songs were "I Forgot to Remember to Forget," "Mystery Train," and "Trying to Get to You." The first two of those songs became the two sides of his next single release. "Mystery Train," Elvis's version of a song by Little Junior Parker, is marked by a little chuckle at the end. Again, Elvis changed the original lyrics.

Master of Promotion

Meanwhile, several things were happening that would propel Elvis's career to the next level. Tom Parker was named a "special advisor" to help promote the singer. He proved to be a master of promotion.

Late in 1955, Parker's negotiating skills helped set up one major deal for Elvis and laid the groundwork for others. On November 21, RCA executives paid Phillips thirty-five thousand dollars to bring Elvis from Sun Records to RCA. They also gave Elvis five thousand dollars as a signing bonus. Today, that seems like a ridiculously low price to buy the contract for the person who would turn out to be arguably the biggest star in the history of popular music. In 1955, however, that figure was regarded as "something decidedly larger than a king's ransom." In fact, it was more than had ever been paid before to buy out a performer's contract.[7]

In many ways, RCA took a risk based on Elvis's potential. At the time, he had very little national recognition. Soon, however, RCA's investment paid off in spectacular fashion.

Meanwhile, Phillips was sorry to lose the star attraction from his record label. However, the deal benefited him as well. He had almost all his resources tied up in Elvis. The cash he received for his star's contract would allow him to work with more artists and help launch other careers. For instance, he was getting ready to release a new Carl Perkins record called "Blue Suede Shoes." That song would become a classic. In fact, Elvis soon recorded it himself.

At the time, Perkins's version proved to be much more popular. Over time that changed. "Inevitably, Perkins was overshadowed by Presley, who eventually made the shoe song his own," wrote Toby Creswell.[8]

Soon after Elvis was signed by RCA, Phillips summed up his feelings this way: "I feel Elvis is one of the most talented youngsters today, and by releasing his contract to RCA-Victor we will give him the opportunity of entering the largest organization of its kind in the world, so his talents can be given the fullest opportunity."[9]

A week later, Elvis sent a thank-you telegram to Parker. In it he said, "I've always known and now my folks are assured that you are the best, most wonderful person I could ever hope to work with. Believe me when I say I will stick with you through thick and thin and do everything I can to uphold your faith in me."[10]

Parker kept pushing on behalf of his client. Even as he worked to close the deal with RCA-Victor, he contacted the William Morris talent agency about having Elvis star in a movie. He likened Elvis to movie star James Dean, who had recently died in an automobile accident. "If you ever follow one of my hunches, follow up on this one and you won't go wrong," Parker said.[11]

Meanwhile, Parker worked to establish exclusive control over Elvis's career. First he went to work on Elvis's parents. He tried to convince them that he could help Elvis take his career to new levels and help him make more money. Vernon agreed right away. Gladys held out. She did not trust him and made that fact clear to both Elvis and Vernon.

Because Elvis was only twenty, he was considered a minor. This meant that both of his parents would have to approve and sign any contracts. Eventually, Parker won Gladys over—at least enough to get her signature. When Neal's contract expired in March 1956, Parker took over as Elvis's exclusive manager, a position he held for the rest of the singer's life. For his efforts, Parker at first received 25 percent of Elvis's total earnings.

How did Neal feel about being eased out? He said he wasn't bothered. "My contract with Elvis was to expire and I simply let it go," he said.[12]

A Year to Remember

Under Parker's shrewd guidance, and using his own great talent, Elvis set out to hit the top. And the year he had in 1956 certainly challenges for the most successful year ever for a recording artist.

On January 10, 1956, Elvis recorded his first song for RCA-Victor. And what a song it was. "Heartbreak Hotel" topped the national popular music charts for an amazing eight weeks beginning in April. It topped the country charts even longer, staying at number one for seventeen weeks. It even reached number five on the rhythm and blues charts. The song made Elvis a national sensation and moved him from being a country star to being a rock-and-roll star.

> "Heartbreak Hotel" topped the national popular music charts for an amazing eight weeks beginning in April 1956.

Ironically, RCA executives at first did not think very highly of the record. With depressing lyrics and unique guitar and piano riffs, the song was unlike other popular songs of the time. Elvis managed to capture the raw emotion of the song perfectly.

On January 28, Elvis appeared on *Stage Show*, a national television show produced by actor Jackie Gleason. The theater in New York City where the show was filmed was not nearly filled. Elvis may have been a star in the South, but the people in New York City did not know him yet. They did after this performance, as did people throughout America.

Elvis jerked and twisted as he sang. According to biographer Jerry Hopkins, "He sneered, dropped his eyelids, and smiled out of the left side of his mouth. He used every physical trick that had come to him in the 16 months since his first record was released."[13]

Soon Elvis also appeared on Milton Berle's popular television show. Ratings skyrocketed, but not everyone was impressed. Ben Gross of the *New York Daily News* wrote that "Elvis's grunt and groin antics were suggestive and vulgar." Another critic dismissed his singing as "caterwauling."[14]

His gyrations while on stage earned him the nickname "Elvis the Pelvis." He found that offensive. "I don't like to be called Elvis the Pelvis," he said. "I mean, it's one of the most childish expressions I've ever heard coming from an adult. Elvis the Pelvis. My pelvis has nothing to do with what I do."[15]

Meanwhile, the Catholic weekly magazine *America* said, "If his 'entertainment' could be confined to records, it might not be too bad an influence on the young, but unfortunately Presley makes personal appearances. . . . If the agencies (TV and other) would stop handling such nauseating stuff, all the Presleys of our land would soon be swallowed in the oblivion they deserve."[16]

Parker, meanwhile, was delighted with the furor. All the attention made Elvis's records sell even faster. The furor reached such heights that Steve Allen made Elvis tone down his performance for *The Steve Allen Show*. Elvis appeared in a white tuxedo and crooned his new song "Hound Dog" to an actual hound dog. Many of Elvis's fans—and Elvis himself—found that presentation demeaning.

In all, Elvis released four chart-topping songs in 1956. In addition to "Heartbreak Hotel," the others were "I Want You, I Need You, I Love You," "Don't Be Cruel/Hound Dog," and "Love Me Tender." Between them, the latter two songs spent sixteen consecutive weeks on the charts. At one point, they were number one and number two. "Love Me Tender" remains one of Elvis's most popular ballads even today.

It was a remarkable run. No other artist would enjoy that type of success until nearly a decade later, when the Beatles held down the top five spots all at once during one magic week in April 1964.

Not only were Elvis's records hot, but so were his television performances. Throughout 1956, he appeared on a variety of national television shows. These culminated with two performances on the wildly popular *Ed Sullivan Show*. He made a third appearance in early 1957. The performances drew huge television audiences and cemented Elvis's stature as an American icon.

Elvis used his newfound riches to provide for the comfort of his family. In 1955, he had moved his parents into a rented house in Memphis. A few months later, he moved them into a larger place in a better part of town. In March 1956, he bought a house in one of the nicest areas of Memphis. He paid forty thousand dollars in cash, a huge sum in those days.

In some ways, the wooden house was similar to the house they had owned on Berry Street in East Tupelo. It was much larger, however. Also, it was a ranch-style house. This meant that Gladys, whose health was declining, would not have to go up and down stairs. Elvis was pleased to be able to make life better for his parents—especially his beloved Gladys.

But as Elvis's fame continued to grow, the Presleys struggled to enjoy their new home. Fans, mostly young women, rang the doorbell at all hours of the day and night hoping to catch a glimpse of their hero. Sometimes crowds of girls hung out on the sidewalk outside waiting for Elvis to enter or to exit the house.

The neighbors in this upscale neighborhood did not like all the commotion. They also did not like the way the Presleys kept their house. Gladys hung her laundry out on the clothesline each day where everyone could see it, and littering the backyard were stacks of wood that she planned to use to set up a chicken coop. Neighbors soon began complaining that having the Presleys around would bring down their property values. Neighbors even filed a public nuisance lawsuit against Elvis. The judge threw out the case.

Not only did Elvis have lots of money, but he also spent it freely. He bought new outfits, many sporting his favorite colors—black and pink. By April 1956, he owned forty suits and twenty-seven pairs of shoes.[17] He bought Gladys a pink Cadillac, even though she didn't like to drive.

> **Still, with his growing fame and money Elvis often found himself unhappy.**

Still, with his growing fame and money Elvis often found himself unhappy. He felt immense pressure. Now that he was on top, he had to work even harder to stay on top. Further, everywhere he went, crowds now followed. This loss of privacy bothered him.

Elvis also struggled to have a meaningful relationship with women, although he continued to sleep with women in many of the towns he visited. During 1955 and 1956, he was linked with several women, including Barbara Hearn, Wanda Jackson, and actress Natalie Wood.

Elvis spent the most time with June Juanico. He and Juanico even went on vacation together to Biloxi, Mississippi. Later in 1956, she went to Hollywood with him. In many ways, they seemed perfectly matched. She said that he proposed to her in the summer of 1956, with the agreement that they would wait a few years until his career was solidly established. In the end, she decided not to wait for him. She married another man in 1957.

Elvis also had to worry that overeager fans might hurt him in their enthusiasm. As the crowds grew larger and rowdier, Elvis hired Red West, a big burly young man he had met in high school to be his bodyguard. By now he needed protection both at concerts and around town from the crowds he attracted. Young women were always trying to touch him. In the furor, people could get hurt. Elvis could get hurt.

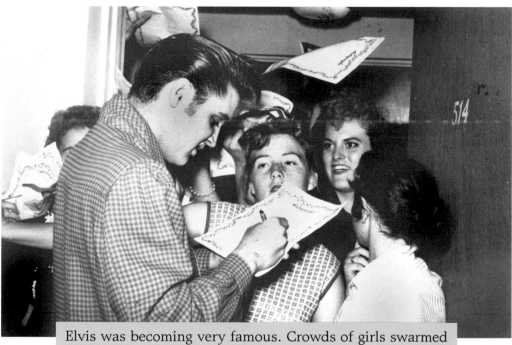

Elvis was becoming very famous. Crowds of girls swarmed him asking for his autograph.

Making Movies

But even as his records continued to climb the charts and his concerts continued to sell out, Elvis also undertook a new challenge. In late March 1956, Parker arranged for Elvis to do a movie screen test for Hal Wallis at Paramount Studios in Hollywood. In early April, Wallis offered a contract for one motion picture with options to make six more.

Shooting began in August for *The Reno Brothers*, the story about three Confederate soldiers who were unaware the Civil War had ended. Elvis played Clint Reno. In the film, Clint got shot and killed. But Elvis did appear again to sing as the closing credits rolled.

Elvis recorded four songs for *The Reno Brothers*. One of them, "Love Me Tender," seemed destined to be a hit. To capitalize on that, the name of the movie was changed to *Love Me Tender*. The film opened in New York City in mid-November. Soon after that the title song, "Love Me Tender," went to number one.

In September Elvis returned to Tupelo, Mississippi, to perform a special homecoming concert for five thousand screaming fans.

Another highlight came in December when Elvis joined Jerry Lee Lewis and Carl Perkins for a late-night jam session at Sun Studios. Johnny Cash also dropped by. All four singers were or had been signed up to the Sun Studios label. The impromptu session became known as the Million Dollar Quartet. All four later went on to be inducted into the Rock and Roll Hall of Fame.

The music, the movies, the image. It was all part of Parker's strategy to build Elvis into the biggest star the world had ever known. Indeed, it took no more than a year for Elvis to become the biggest-selling artist in the music business and the highest-paid performer on TV.

> **The music, the movies, the image. It was all part of Colonel Tom Parker's strategy to build Elvis into the biggest star the world had ever known.**

Parker even turned Elvis into a brand name, licensing seventy-eight different products, ranging from Elvis charm bracelets to glow-in-the-dark busts over the years. In 1956 alone, sales of Elvis-related items totaled $22 million.[18]

"No artist had ever exploded on the scene with the volcanic impact of Elvis Presley in 1956, and no manager before Tom Parker had ever been so brilliantly, or blatantly, capitalistic," wrote Elvis biographer Nash. "At a time when most managers did little more for their artists than book concert dates, Parker perpetually figured out new ways to exploit his star."[19]

The strategy paid off. In October 1956, *Variety* magazine dubbed Elvis "the King of Rock 'n' Roll"—a nickname that would stick with him throughout his life.[20]

As 1956 ended, Elvis stood atop the world. What would come next?

Chapter 7

The King Reigns

How do you follow up the biggest year in the history of entertainment? Elvis Presley followed with another year that was just as big. Once again he charted four number-one hits: "Too Much," "All Shook Up," "(Let Me Be Your) Teddy Bear," and "Jailhouse Rock/Treat Me Nice." Together, those records spent an amazing twenty-five weeks atop the charts—almost half the year.

The song "Teddy Bear" had an amusing origin. Somehow the rumor started that Elvis collected teddy bears. He didn't really, but fans did not know that. Soon people all over the world were sending him teddy bears. Based on that, songwriters Kal Mann and Bernie Lowe were inspired to write "Teddy Bear" for the Elvis film *Loving You*.

In addition to producing hit records, Elvis made two popular movies in 1957. In *Loving You*, he played a fame-bound hillbilly singer. According to writer/director Hal Kanter, "*Loving You* was probably a more realistic view of the Elvis persona, his life and his style, than any film that he made after that."[1]

Elvis's performance won over some critics of his acting. Jim Powers of the *Hollywood Reporter* didn't like Elvis in *Love Me Tender*. He thought the performance in *Loving You* was much better. "Presley . . . acts naturally and with appeal," Powers wrote.[2]

In *Jailhouse Rock*, Elvis played an ex-convict who becomes a rock star. Despite decidedly mixed reviews, *Jailhouse Rock* was a big success. The film peaked at number three on the movie charts. The hard-driving song "Jailhouse Rock" did even better, spending seven weeks atop the music charts. The song-and-dance number that opens the film takes place in jail. Elvis helped choreograph the number himself, and it is probably the most famous scene from any of his movies. "Many modern-day music critics cite the sequence as the blueprint and inspiration for the music video genre," wrote Adam Victor.[3]

The King Finds His Castle

Probably the biggest highlight of the year for the King of Rock and Roll was finding his castle. Eager to find a more secluded home where they could escape the legions of fans, Vernon and Gladys Presley began searching throughout Memphis. Soon they found a mansion on the outskirts of Memphis that seemed suitable. Named Graceland after the great-aunt of the woman whom it was built for, the house was

> **Probably the biggest highlight of the year for the King of Rock and Roll was finding his castle.**

A film still from 1957's *Jailhouse Rock*. Elvis is center, standing on the floor.

set in a grove of oak trees. The fourteen-acre property seemed ideal, and on March 16, 1957, Elvis's parents called him in Hollywood, where he was filming, to tell him about it.

On March 25, the Presleys purchased Graceland at a cost of $102,500. That figure represented a small fortune for a house in those days. The average annual wage in the United States in 1957 was $3,641.72.[4]

Buying Graceland also seemed to perk Gladys up. For awhile, she enjoyed decorating the family's new home. Soon, however, she felt as caged at Graceland as she had in their previous home. Fans hung around outside the estate's fence at all hours of the day and night, hoping for a glimpse of Elvis on those occasions when he wasn't touring. She soon told a friend, "I'm miserable. I'm guarded. I can't go buy my own groceries. I can't go to the movies. I can't see my neighbors. I'm the most miserable woman in the world."[5]

Concerts, Movies, and More

Right after buying Graceland, Elvis returned to the road. After a brief tour, Elvis headed back to Hollywood to film *Jailhouse Rock*. Although he never formally studied acting, each evening he carefully reviewed his performance from that day. He analyzed what he was doing and looked for ways to make it better. "I always criticize myself in films," he told one interviewer. "I'm always striving to be natural in front of a camera. That takes studying, of a sort."[6]

While he was filming *Jailhouse Rock*, Elvis had to defend himself against a rumor that he had made racist remarks. According to the rumor, Elvis had said that black people were good only for buying his records and shining his shoes. Elvis denied the rumor, saying, "I never said anything like that, and people who know me know I wouldn't have said it." He added that he admired black culture and black singers.[7]

On July 3, he learned that Judy Tyler, his love interest in *Jailhouse Rock*, had died in an automobile accident. Elvis was devastated. He did not attend the funeral. He feared that his attendance would disrupt the service.

One major irony in *Jailhouse Rock* is that Elvis's character has killed someone. Over the course of the movie he serves time in prison and then becomes a rock star when he is released. Record companies and

Hollywood welcome him with open arms. Meanwhile, Elvis, who was really pretty clean-cut, found his records banned in many places. Some religious leaders and parents found rock-and-roll music objectionable.

An essayist in the *Catholic Sun* called Elvis's music a "voodoo of frustration and defiance." And the *New York Daily News* described rock and roll in general as "a barrage of primitive jungle-beat rhythm set to lyrics which few adults would care to hear."[8]

> **Elvis, who was really pretty clean-cut, found his records banned in many places.**

Some established recording artists criticized the rock-and-roll movement as well. Frank Sinatra declared that rock and roll was "phoney [sic] and false" and sung by "goons." Asked for a response to Sinatra's comments, Elvis politely disagreed with the older singer. "He has a right to say what he wants to say," Elvis stated. "He is a great success and a fine actor, but I think he shouldn't have said it. He's mistaken about this. This is a trend, just the same as he faced when he started years ago."[9]

In September Elvis and his band embarked on a brief tour of the northwestern United States and Vancouver, Canada. Later that month he returned to Tupelo for a special benefit show. Some twelve thousand people attended the show. The money raised supported the planned Elvis Presley Youth Center. The concert was a triumph. However, when Elvis returned to Tupelo a few years later he found that the center had not been built. No one knows what happened to the money that had been raised.

More than fifty years later, in 2008, the Tupelo Elvis Presley Fan Club convinced the Mississippi Legislature to approve a specialty Elvis license plate. Proceeds will go to support the youth center, wrote Chris Talbott of the Associated Press. It was always Elvis's wish "to take care of the east side of town where he grew up," said club president Scott Reese.[10]

In October 1957, *Elvis' Christmas Album* was released. The record ran into problems. Irving Berlin, whose rendition of "White Christmas" is considered a classic, asked radio stations not to play Elvis's version. He believed the Elvis rendition went against the spirit of Christmas. Nonetheless, the album reached the top of the charts. It sold well at holiday time for years to come.

On October 28, Elvis performed for the first time in Hollywood. A sellout crowd went wild at his first show. Not everyone approved, however. Dick Williams of the *Los Angeles Mirror-News* wrote, "If any further proof were needed that what Elvis offers is not basically music but a sex show, it was proved last night." Furthermore, the Los Angeles Vice Squad told Tom Parker that Elvis needed to tone down the show for the second night. Otherwise he might go to jail for indecency. The police actually showed up with movie cameras to film the second show. If Elvis did anything obscene, they would have proof on tape. The show that night was much tamer, however.

Next, Elvis made his first trip to Hawaii, where he performed two shows. That stop, too, was a huge success. Still, all was not rosy for Elvis. Scotty Moore and Bill Black quit as his band members that fall. They felt they were not being paid enough. They each earned a hundred dollars a week at home and two hundred a week while on the road, but they had to pay all their own traveling expenses.

"Elvis is the star, and we know it," Scotty was quoted as saying at the time. "I didn't expect to get rich on this . . . but I did expect to do better than I have and to make a good living for my family."[11] The boys did come back and play on a day-by-day basis sometimes as needed, but it was never the same after that.

Also, Elvis seemed to feel a vague disquiet about his performing. The concerts still exuded raw power. They still drew hordes of screaming fans. But Elvis sensed something was missing—at least for him. "There was nothing new," wrote biographer Peter Guralnick. "It was all something he had done before. . . . For the first time in a long time he was no longer sure what was supposed to happen next."[12]

Elvis felt the same discomfort when he got back to Memphis. He told the Reverend James Hamill, "I am the most miserable young man you have ever seen. I have got more money than I can ever spend. I have thousands of fans out there, and I have a lot of people who call themselves my friends, but I am miserable."[13]

Elvis seemed to feel a vague disquiet about his performing.

Actually, Elvis had more than thousands of fans. He had millions. Many of them organized fan clubs for their hero. Marion Keisker of Sun Records set up the first one just weeks after Elvis recorded his first single. As his fame spread, similar clubs formed across the world. By 1956, Elvis received an astounding ten thousand letters a week. Of course, he could personally read only a few of them.

As Elvis's star continued to rise, Gladys's health continued to decline. Even after the move to Graceland, she felt the lack of privacy. She could not go out in public without being noticed. She constantly worried about how she looked. Furthermore, she worried about Elvis whenever he traveled. "He was supposed to phone last night and he didn't," she would tell her sister Lillian. "I know something bad's happened to him."[14]

To forget her troubles, Gladys turned to liquor. She also took diet pills. Together, the two took a heavy toll on her health. "From about July [1957] on, Gladys just seemed to lose interest in everything," recalled Lillian. "Elvis was always buying animals for them, but she had no time for any of them, except the chickens and the little Boston bulldog he gave her."[15]

Elvis Is Drafted

All of Elvis's success with his records, his movies, and his tours could not prevent him from facing the same fate as thousands of other young people across the United States—being drafted. At the time, there were not enough volunteers to fill the needed slots in the U.S. armed services. Therefore, young men registered for the draft when they turned eighteen and went into the service if and when their name was drawn by the draft board.

To get away from adoring fans who would ring the door bell day and night, Elvis found Graceland. Here, Elvis stands in front of Graceland in 1958.

In mid-December 1957, the Memphis Draft Board let it be known that Elvis would soon receive his draft notice. Almost immediately, the army, navy, and air force contacted him. If he volunteered before he was drafted, he could pick his branch of the service and possibly even the type of work he would do. Each offered him a special deal.

For instance, the army offered Elvis a role in its Special Services branch. There he would travel around and entertain the troops. Manager Parker refused to even consider it. "If they want my boy to sing," he said, "they are going to have to pay for it like anyone else."[16]

Instead, Elvis was drafted into the army as a regular soldier. The two-year commitment threatened his wildly successful career. Fans are fickle. Tastes change quickly. During the two years Elvis would be away, his fans might transfer their allegiance to other singers.

> **In mid-December 1957, the Memphis Draft Board let it be known that Elvis would soon receive his draft notice.**

Still, Parker saw potential advantages. He thought army service would transform Presley's image and make him an even bigger star. Elvis "would look like a hero," noted Parker biographer Alanna Nash. "And when he got out two years later, he would be visibly tamed, transformed into a pure symbol of America, a clean-cut god for the masses."[17]

Elvis took the news of his impending army service well. In fact, at Christmastime in 1957 he let photographers come to Graceland and take pictures of him with his draft notice under the Christmas tree. Talking to reporters, Elvis said that he would miss his mother and father while in the service. He added, however, that "I'm kind-a proud of it. It's a duty I've got to fill and I'm gonna do it."[18]

Parker insisted to Elvis that he should be treated like everyone else in the army. Elvis agreed. He did ask for one accommodation, though. He was scheduled to begin filming his next movie, *King Creole*, in January. On the day before Christmas, Elvis wrote a letter to the draft board asking for a deferment—or postponement—in the date of his induction so that the movie could be shot. He was not asking for himself, he noted, but on behalf of Paramount, "so these folks will not lose so much money, with everything they have done so far."[19]

The draft board agreed to grant Elvis a sixty-day deferment. This meant that he would be inducted on March 20 rather than in January.

Elvis returned to Hollywood in January to film *King Creole*. By this time, he traveled with an entourage of nearly a dozen people. He had gathered a group of friends to help him with various things, from driving his car to serving as his bodyguard. The innermost members of this group became known as the Memphis Mafia.

King Creole tells the story of a singer who works as a busboy in a bar called King Creole on Bourbon Street in New Orleans. The movie also starred Carolyn Jones, Walter Matthau, Vic Morrow, Brian Hutton, and Dolores Hart. *King Creole* remained Elvis's personal favorite of all the films he was to make.

The movie also drew favorable reviews. Paul Dehn, in the British publication *New Chronicle*, wrote, "The part gives him scope to stop acting like an electrocuted baboon and to act like a human being, which he does with a new skill, a new restraint and a new charm." *The New York Times* simply ran a headline that said, "Elvis can act!"[20]

After the movie was finished filming, Elvis had just ten days to spend at Graceland before entering the army. He spent time with his parents and friends and got ready to go. As he prepared to enter this new phase of his life, he wondered if his career would still be alive when he finished.

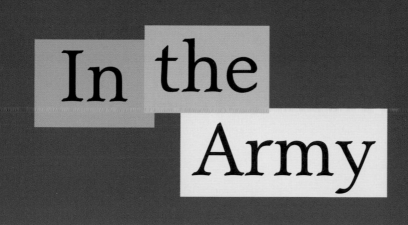

Chapter 8

In the
Army

Like almost everything involving twenty-three-year-old Elvis Presley, his induction into the U.S. Army on March 24, 1958, became a media circus. Elvis arrived at his local draft board at 6:35 A.M. Even at that early hour, a horde of reporters and photographers were waiting for him.

Gladys Presley, despite her ill health, looked better than she had in quite some time. She appeared somber, yet composed as her beloved son prepared to begin army life. She emerged as a "figure of dignity."[1]

That afternoon, Elvis and a dozen other recruits boarded a bus bound for Fort Chaffee, Arkansas. The next day, fifty-five reporters and photographers watched as barber James Peterson gave Elvis the traditional army crew cut. Elvis caught some of the falling hair, and quipped, "Hair today, gone tomorrow."[2] Asked about his new barracks buddies, Elvis responded, "They've been swell to me. They treat me like anyone else, though. That's the way I want it."[3]

Elvis (center) and his parents on the day he reported to U.S. Army duty.

Next Elvis reported to Fort Hood, Texas. There he completed eight weeks of basic training, followed by fourteen weeks of more specialized training. He settled into army life fairly easily. Unlike some recruits, he didn't mind rising early. "There's not much difference between this and making a movie," he said. "In Hollywood, you have to get up at 5 A.M. and be on the set at 6. The only different thing here is that you don't have a limousine."[4]

Thanks to the efforts of Tom Parker, all of Elvis's training activities were captured by the media. Others cashed in on the media frenzy as well. Many artists recorded "tribute" songs, such as "Bye, Bye Elvis" by Gennie Harris and "Marchin' Elvis" by the Greats. Soon a play appeared on Broadway titled *Bye Bye Birdie*, about a rock-and-roll singer named Conrad Birdie who goes into the army. It quickly became a hit, at least partly because of Elvis.

Elvis tried hard to be a good soldier. Officers and other soldiers alike admired his positive attitude and work ethic. His fans vowed not to forget him while he was in the army. In fact, he received fifteen thousand letters a week while he was at Fort Hood. All of the letters were forwarded to Parker's office in Madison, Tennessee.

The Death of Gladys

Probably the biggest adjustment for Elvis was being out of touch with his mother. Even when he toured, he could call home whenever he wished. During basic training, he did not have the same opportunities. In this era before cell phones, there were only a few phones on base. Most were restricted for official army use only. Finally, after two weeks Elvis had a chance to call his mother. For the next hour, recalled his friend Eddie Fadal, "they were crying and moaning on the telephone—hardly a word was spoken."[5]

> **Probably the biggest adjustment for Elvis was being out of touch with his mother.**

Elvis received a furlough to visit home in late May and early June. He brought his army friend Rex Mansfield to stay with him in Graceland. While home, Elvis attended a preview of his new movie, *King Creole*. He also traveled to Nashville for a recording session—his last for the next two years. From that session came future hits, including "A Big Hunk o' Love," "A Fool Such as I," and "I Need Your Love Tonight." Those songs kept Elvis's music in the public eye—and ear—while he was in the army.

Soldiers who had family nearby were allowed to move out of the barracks. Therefore, when Elvis returned to Fort Hood, he rented a three-bedroom trailer home. Then Gladys and Vernon Presley joined him, along with Vernon's mother, Minnie, and Elvis's friend Lamar Fike. Soon after, they moved to a house where they had more room.

While in Texas, Gladys's condition continued to decline. Years of drinking and taking diet pills had taken their toll on her body. The first week in August, she went to the doctor. Her skin was jaundiced, or yellow, but the local doctor could not determine a cause. On Friday, August 8, she climbed on a train back home to Memphis. The next day she went into the hospital. The doctors said she had hepatitis. This is an inflammation of the liver. Serious cases can be fatal. At first, however, doctors said that Gladys was very ill but that her condition did not seem life threatening.

Each day, however, her condition grew worse. On Tuesday, August 12, Elvis asked for emergency leave to go to her. He threatened to go AWOL (absent without leave) if he did not receive a pass. He arrived in Memphis that evening. By this time, her condition was critical.

Elvis stayed at his mother's bedside for a full day. On Wednesday evening she told him to go back to Graceland and get some sleep, so he did. But during the night, Elvis got a call from the hospital. He raced to the hospital, but Gladys had already died. Elvis was heartbroken. "He could not stop stroking her body and calling for her to come back," wrote Elvis biographer Marie Clayton.[6]

Doctors listed the cause of death as a heart attack. Gladys's body was taken to Graceland. As the news spread, a crowd gathered outside the gates. Elvis should have been able to grieve his mother's death privately. Instead, the funeral became a public spectacle. After that experience, Elvis always felt suspicious of the media.

At first the funeral was to be held at Graceland. At the last minute, however, it was moved to downtown Memphis. It took sixty-five police cars to escort the procession of mourners to the cemetery. Elvis paid to have Gladys's favorite group, the Blackwood Brothers, sing at the funeral.

Elvis had been extremely close to his mother. Her death hit him hard. He cried throughout much of the funeral. "Everything I have is gone," he wailed.[7]

Elvis's Aunt Lillian believed he never fully recovered from his mother's death. After Gladys died, "[h]e changed completely," she said.[8]

Off to Germany

Still, life went on. Elvis returned to his army training in Texas. Several members of his entourage moved into his off-base house to help keep his spirits up. Soon he prepared to ship out for his assignment to West Germany. In the late 1950s, Germany was divided into two parts. East Germany had a communist government. It was backed by the Soviet Union. West Germany was a democracy. It was backed by the United States and its allies.

Elvis had been extremely close to his mother. Her death hit him hard.

Elvis heads off to boot camp in 1958.

On September 22, 1958, Elvis gave a farewell press conference in New York. Then he climbed aboard the USS *General George M. Randall* as a military band played a medley of his rock-and-roll hits. He said that while he would be out of his fan's sight for awhile, "I hope I'm not out of their minds."[9]

Elvis arrived in West Germany on October 1. Swarms of fans came to meet the ship, and he gave another press conference the following day. Then he was assigned his duty as a jeep driver on an army base in the town of Friedberg.

To help him feel less lonely, Elvis paid for his father and his grandmother Minnie to travel to Germany, along with his friends Red West and Lamar Fike. Given permission to move off base, Elvis and his group lived in a hotel for awhile. They soon got in trouble with the manager for setting off fireworks and making too much noise. Finally, they set a small fire while fooling around one day. Smoke filtered out into the hall, and the manager asked them to leave. Then they moved into the house of a woman named Frau Pieper in the town of Bad Nauheim. They stayed there the rest of Elvis's time in Germany.

At the insistence of his manager, Elvis refused to perform in public for the troops during his time in Germany, although he was often asked. Parker would not allow him to perform for free, even for the army. Besides, Elvis simply wanted to do his job as a soldier. "We've asked him and he said, 'I'd rather not, sir,'" said Major General Thomas F. Van Natta. "I think he feels he has an obligation to his country and he wants to pay it like everyone else and get it over with. . . . He's a good soldier."[10]

Parker would not allow him to perform for free, even for the army.

Indeed, Elvis continued to serve faithfully throughout his time in Germany. By early 1960, he had been promoted to the rank of sergeant. "Since his arrival, Presley has demonstrated leadership ability and proved himself worthy of promotion of sergeant," said Captain Hubert Childress, his company commander.[11]

Elvis often won awards for "Best Dressed Soldier." One reason was that his friends always kept his brass and boots shined to perfection. He had about "eight or ten pairs of boots and probably a hundred uniforms, a hundred shirts, a hundred pants," recalled friend Lamar. He also always had a nice car on hand for field trips as time permitted.[12]

Still, Elvis worked hard in the army. He trained and marched like all the other soldiers. He went on maneuvers with his unit near the border of what was then Czechoslovakia.

It may have been then that Elvis began taking amphetamines. These are pills that help people keep awake and alert for long periods. At the time, no prescription was needed to get amphetamines. Many soldiers took them. However, for Elvis the pills posed special problems. He already had trouble sleeping, as he had much of his life. Taking pills that further disrupted his sleep patterns only made things worse.

> **It may have been then that Elvis began taking amphetamines.**

While stationed in Germany, Elvis kept himself busy in many ways while off duty. He often played football with other soldiers and with local youths. He also began to take up karate, which remained an interest throughout his life. Karate helped him focus his energy in positive ways.

Meanwhile, back home Elvis's records continued to sell well. Periodically, RCA would release some of the new songs Elvis had recorded before he left. RCA also repackaged some of his previously released records.

At the same time, Parker negotiated new movie deals for Elvis. That way he could pick up his film career as soon as he earned his discharge from the army. He also continued to earn money from his previous films. Indeed, Parker estimated that Elvis earned $2 million in 1958. This was an amazing amount in those days, especially considering that Elvis had spent most of the year in the service.[13]

Finding Time for Romance

Elvis also made time for romance while in Germany. While out on maneuvers, he met nineteen-year-old

Elisabeth Stefaniak. The two dated for awhile. When he returned to Bad Nauheim, she went along to serve as his secretary. But Elisabeth soon learned that she and Janie Wilbanks, another girlfriend from the same period, were "only two peas in a big pod full of girls."[14]

Elvis had many other girlfriends while in Germany, including Vera Tschechowa, a beautiful eighteen-year-old German starlet who had been voted Germany's number-one pinup girl that year. That meant that more of her posters had been sold than those of any other female celebrity in Germany. Meanwhile, he also kept in touch from time to time with Anita Wood, his girlfriend back home.

However, Elvis's most intriguing romance was with dark-haired beauty Priscilla Ann Beaulieu. The stepdaughter of U.S. Air Force Captain Joseph Paul Beaulieu, Priscilla and her family moved to Germany in July 1959. She and Elvis were introduced through an airman named Currie Grant.

Twenty-four-year-old Elvis and Priscilla felt an immediate spark toward each other and started spending time together. However, Priscilla was only fourteen years old, and she lived about an hour away in the town of Wiesbaden. On their fourth date, her stepfather insisted on meeting Elvis. He grilled Elvis about his intentions.

Elvis turned on the charm. Noting that Priscilla was very mature for her age, he talked about how lonely he was stationed so far from home. "I guess you might say I need someone to talk

> **Elvis's most intriguing romance was with dark-haired beauty Priscilla Ann Beaulieu.**

to," Elvis said. "You don't need to worry about her, Captain. I'll take good care of her."[15]

Captain Beaulieu allowed the two to date under the condition that they have a chaperone. Soon she was spending more and more evenings at Elvis's house. She understood that Elvis saw other women, but she accepted that.

Despite the special place she held in Elvis's heart, Priscilla worried about the many other girls who wanted him. Press reports also continued to link him with former Memphis girlfriend Anita Wood. Still, his relationship with Priscilla lasted throughout his stay in Germany.

Elvis felt safe talking with Priscilla about his innermost thoughts. "I really felt I got to know who Elvis Presley was during this time," she later said. "He was his most vulnerable, his most honest, I would say his most passionate during that time."[16]

Elvis's tour of duty in Germany was slated to end in early 1960. His discharge from the army proved to be just as much of a media circus as his induction. Journalists from around the world were on hand for his press conference on March 1. They asked him a number of questions, including about his relationship with Priscilla.

"She's about 16, but she's very mature for her years," Presley said. "I'm very fond of her, but she's just a friend. There's no big romance."[17]

Elvis was not being fully truthful. In reality, Priscilla was not yet even fifteen, and the two had certainly had a romance going. Elvis and Priscilla had spent many evenings in his bedroom, talking and kissing. The night before he was to return to the United States, "I begged him to consummate our love," she later recalled. Elvis declined. He thought she was too young for that.[18]

On March 2, 1960, Elvis and Priscilla shared a tearful farewell before he boarded the plane back to the United States. He promised to call as soon as he got home. He even gave her his combat jacket as a token that she belonged to him.

Would Elvis resume life as the world's biggest rock and roll star? Or would his fans have moved on to other musical tastes? He would soon find out.

Chapter 9

Back on Top, But for How Long?

If Elvis Presley had worried his fans had forgotten him, those fears were quickly put to rest. On his train ride home, hundreds of fans gathered with welcome home signs at each stop. When he arrived in Memphis, the police had to escort him to Graceland. They whisked him through the crowd without stopping to chat or sign autographs.

Within a couple of weeks, Elvis and his entourage took a chartered bus to Nashville, where he had his first recording session as a civilian. Working overnight, he completed a new single called "Stuck on You/Fame and Fortune" and four other songs to be used on an upcoming album. Scotty Moore and D. J. Fortuna joined him for the session, as did the Jordanaires, Colonel Tom Parker, and some local musicians. To avoid an avalanche of fans, top-secret conditions prevailed. To help ensure that word about the session did not leak out, the local musicians were told they would be working with another artist, not Elvis.

Fans could hardly wait for Elvis's first post-army record. They placed more than 1.2 million advance orders before the song had even been recorded. "Stuck on You," a mellow pop song, reached number one in less than a month and remained there for four weeks. The King of Rock and Roll had regained his crown.

Still, not all was rosy for Elvis. He strongly disapproved of his father's decision to marry Dee Stanley, the woman Vernon had started dating in Germany. In fact, Elvis did not even attend the wedding. Vernon and Dee moved into Graceland along with Dee's three boys.

Elvis welcomed them as best he could, but his mind was focused on Hollywood. "More than anything, I want to be an actor," he said, "the kind that stays around for a long time."[1]

Movie Machine

Producer Hal Wallis put Elvis right back to work in a movie called *G.I. Blues*. The film was designed to cash in on Elvis's time in the army and featured eleven songs. Critics called the plot weak and the song selection tepid. Indeed, the film marked the beginning of a downward spiral for Elvis's film career. Over the next nine years, he made twenty-seven movies. Most were panned by movie critics, but most made money for the film companies. However, their overall low quality undercut any hope Elvis had of being taken seriously as an actor.

The basic template for an Elvis movie included "girls, songs, and gorgeous locations." He generally had a

Over the next nine years, he made twenty-seven movies.

85

In the early 1960s, Elvis performed in many movies. This film still is from *Blue Hawaii*.

"manly" occupation—but one that allowed him to break into song at key points. Still, the movies were enormously popular—at least at first—as were the hit songs and albums that came from them.[2]

Along the way, Elvis played a boxer (in *Kid Galahad*), a singer running a charter fishing service (in *Girls! Girls! Girls!*), look-alike relations (in *Kissin' Cousins*), a carnival worker (in *Roustabout*), a pilot (*Paradise, Hawaiian Style*), a race car driver (in *Spinout*), the manager of a traveling medicine show (in *The Trouble With Girls*), and a doctor (in *Change of Habit*). But, over time, even his die-hard fans began to tire of the weak plots and tired scripts.

Some of his roles did give Elvis a chance to show his range as an actor. He really enjoyed his dramatic role as a nightclub singer in *King Creole*, and the movie still stands as one of his best. Likewise, his role as a half-blood Kiowa in *Flaming Star* showed off his dramatic abilities. He even received an award for his positive portrayal of an American Indian.

Other than *Jailhouse Rock*, many people consider *Viva Las Vegas* to be Elvis's best musical role. He had great chemistry with costar Ann-Margret, possibly because the two were dating in real life at the time. *Viva Las Vegas* ranked as the top-grossing film of Elvis's movie career, and it drew critical acclaim as well.

However, with only a few exceptions, the quality of Elvis's movies seemed to decline as the decade of the 1960s wore on. Critic Pauline Kael summed it up this way: "He starred in thirty-one movies, which ranged from mediocre to putrid, and just about in that order."[3]

Another writer noted that, together, the movies "cast an eerie shadow across his life. In his prime as a vocalist and performer, he was condemned to waste almost a decade on ventures that were nothing more than artistic fluff." Indeed, his focus on movie making ended up "effectively sabotaging his previous career as a recording artist and live performer."[4]

Trying to Stay on Top

Still, Elvis remained a strong music presence—at least for awhile. In May 1960, he appeared on a Frank Sinatra television special. Parker demanded and got one hundred twenty-five thousand dollars for Elvis to appear on camera for just a few minutes. For the show, Elvis wore a tuxedo and stood still while singing—no hip swinging. The show garnered huge ratings, but the critics were harsh. One said, "Although Elvis became a sergeant in the Army, as a singer he never left the awkward squad."[5]

Immediately after taping the Sinatra special, Elvis returned to Nashville. There, in one long session, he recorded the twelve songs for his *Elvis Is Back* album, which was released just a week later. Elvis aficionado John Robertson called it "the perfect Presley album" in that "it encapsulated within 12 songs everything that Elvis had been and meant during the Fifties and everything that he would become across the following decade."[6]

The album mixed gritty blues, sizzling sensuality, and powerful pop sounds. "It was a brilliant record, which suggested that nothing was beyond his grasp," wrote Robertson. "It conjured up the vision of a performer who could be all things to all men (and women)."[7]

Unfortunately, most of his subsequent album releases in the 1960s failed to live up to this promise. Between the time Elvis returned from the army and the airing of his landmark TV special in December 1968, RCA issued twenty-three Elvis Presley albums. Fifteen were movie soundtracks. Two more were compilations of previously recorded material. Only six represented original material.

None of these twenty-three albums contained the raucous rock and roll for which he had first gained fame in the 1950s. Many featured a mix of ballads, pop, and soft rock. Elvis could still mesmerize listeners with his talented voice. Love songs such as "Are You Lonesome Tonight?" and "Can't Help Falling in Love" remain classics fifty years after their release.

Still, many fans began to feel that he had lost the "edge" that had first launched him to stardom. His albums and singles continued to sell well, but he no longer dominated the charts. Indeed, between "Good Luck Charm" in 1962 and "Suspicious Minds" in 1969 he endured a period of seven years without a number-one song.

Elvis remained beloved and popular, but a new "generation" of musicians rose to the top in the early to mid-1960s. First and foremost were the Beatles, who launched a string of number-one hits that rivaled Elvis and who, for one magical week in April 1964, held all five top spots on Billboard's charts.

Many fans began to feel that he had lost the "edge" that had first launched him to stardom.

Still, if Elvis felt threatened by groups such as the Beatles, he didn't show it. He sent them a congratulatory telegram before they first appeared on *The Ed Sullivan Show* in 1964. Then in 1965 he invited the Beatles to visit him. He was relaxing in Bel-Air, California, after filming *Blue Hawaii*. The Beatles were in the midst of an American tour.

The meeting of superstars started awkwardly. For awhile, everyone sat around with little to say. But finally they unwound, played music together, and had a good time. "Long live the King!" bellowed Beatle member John Lennon as the group left.[8]

Elvis and His Entourage

From early on during his touring days, Elvis surrounded himself with a group of friends who traveled with him wherever he went. Over the years, some members of the entourage came and went. Others were with him for most of his twenty-year career. Over the years, as many as fifty different people were part of the group at one time or another. Generally, however, he traveled with only a few at a time.

Some of the members included people Elvis had known in high school, such as Red West and George Klein. West had once rescued Elvis from a gang of tough kids in high school, and he became Elvis's bodyguard. West's cousin Sonny also became part of the group. Klein had been Elvis's friend since eighth grade. Elvis would point to Klein in the school photo that hung on the wall at Graceland and say, "He was one of the few guys that was nice to me in school." Two of Klein's friends, Alan Fortas and Marty Lacker, also joined the entourage.[9]

Some other members of the entourage were relatives. Elvis's cousins, Gene Smith, Billy Smith, and Junior Smith were all part of the team for awhile. Junior died in early 1961. Meanwhile, group members Charlie Hodge and Joe Esposito had become close friends with Elvis while serving in the army together. Hodge worked with Elvis for seventeen years, and Esposito served as the "foreman" of the entourage. Lamar Fike was simply a fan who got to meet his idol and managed to become his friend. Fike's loyalty to Elvis led him to try to enlist in the army the same day Elvis was drafted, but he was turned down because he was very overweight.

Because they sometimes carried briefcases and often dressed in black, his entourage earned the nickname "Memphis Mafia." They served as drivers or bodyguards and performed all sorts of other duties as needed. Over time, their motto became "TCB," or "Taking Care of Business." That business involved taking care of Elvis's needs at any hour of the day or night. Elvis even designed a group emblem with the slogan and a picture of a lightning bolt.

The group was on call twenty-four hours a day every day. Because of his strange sleeping habits, Elvis might wake up members of the group in the middle of the night to play racquetball, watch a movie, eat a heavy snack, or even fly off to Las Vegas on a whim. Sometimes Elvis would rent out an entire amusement park, movie theater, or roller rink for an evening so that he and his friends could relax without being disturbed by overeager fans.

> **Their motto became "TCB," or "Taking Care of Business."**

Members of the Memphis Mafia accompanied Elvis when he filmed movies. When he was home at Graceland, they stayed at or near his side. Some of them actually lived on the grounds of the estate. Often, Elvis and his entourage would play intense games of football on the grounds of Graceland. There was only one main rule—Elvis had to win. His entourage made sure he did.

Most of all, the people in his entourage were friends with whom Elvis could hang out and relax after a day of filming or a night of performing. For Elvis, wrote biographer Peter Guralnick, the Memphis Mafia represented "a group of guys with whom he could be comfortable and share some laughs and not have to worry about who he was or where he fit in."[10]

Elvis once said in an interview that he did not like to be alone. With the Memphis Mafia around, that was never a problem. Members of the entourage received a minimal salary, but all their expenses were covered. Plus, they received many fringe benefits. They got to mix and mingle with movie stars. They got to stay in luxurious hotels. In addition, Elvis sometimes surprised them with gifts such as cars or gold jewelry. On more than one occasion, Elvis went on a car-buying binge in which he might buy a dozen or more cars and then give them to family members, his entourage, and other friends.

A Generous Nature

Indeed, Elvis was famed for his generosity. Friends might receive cars or money for no apparent reason. Even a stranger might receive a car or financial help. For instance, one time on a plane in 1970, Elvis gave five hundred dollars (all the cash he was carrying) to a Vietnam veteran who was on the same plane. Another time he purchased an expensive wheelchair for a Memphis woman he had read about in the newspaper (and gave her daughter a car).

In addition, Elvis donated money to a number of charities in Memphis. He also donated fifty thousand dollars to the Motion Picture Relief Fund. This fund helps people in the entertainment field who are having hard times financially.

Elvis did charity concerts as well. Probably the most famous came in Hawaii in March 1961. Elvis performed before a crowd of fifty-five hundred people to raise money toward a memorial to recognize the USS *Arizona*. That battleship had been sunk during the Japanese attack on Pearl Harbor in 1941. The audience responded to his concert with "celebratory whoops and cheers," and the event raised more than fifty thousand dollars.[11]

Elvis and His Women

Talented. Handsome. Wealthy. Elvis ranked as one of the world's most eligible bachelors throughout much of the 1960s. Wherever he went, women threw themselves at him. Elvis did not hesitate to take advantage of these opportunities, even during times when he was dating someone he considered special. For instance, although he remained romantically involved with Anita Wood for several years in the early 1960s, he dated many other women over that same time period.

Elvis enjoyed spending time with women—lots of women. Sometimes he wanted sex. In fact, some nights he had sex with multiple women in the same night. Sometimes he just wanted companionship. He did not like to sleep alone.

Interestingly, Elvis had sex with hundreds of women he met in his travels. He did not, however, have sex with women he really cared about. He told early flame June Juanico that he did not want sexual intercourse with her because he wanted to marry her. Likewise, he once told Elisabeth Stefaniak in Germany that he did not have intercourse with girls he saw regularly because he did not want to risk having them become pregnant.

Meanwhile, Elvis was linked with or actually dated several of his movie costars. These included Tuesday Weld, Juliet Prowse, Yvonne Craig, and others. Probably the most famous and most serious was Ann-Margret. Elvis starred with her in *Viva Las Vegas*. The two seemed perfectly suited to one another. In the end, however, "she fell short on Elvis' conviction that a wife should stay at home and not pursue a career," wrote Adam Victor.[12]

Through it all, however, Priscilla Beaulieu remained in Elvis's heart. For two years after returning home from Germany, he kept in touch sporadically, as his schedule permitted. Then in mid-1962, he invited her to join him in California while he filmed a movie.

Priscilla's stepfather did not think much of this idea. Finally, however, Elvis convinced him. He assured Captain Beaulieu that seventeen-year-old Priscilla would be fully chaperoned during her entire visit. She promised that she would write home each day. As soon as she arrived, however, Elvis took her to Las Vegas. Before they left Hollywood, she pre-drafted a series of postcards. One of Elvis's friends mailed one each day, postmarked in Hollywood. That way, her parents would not be suspicious.

The visit went so well that he invited her to spend the Christmas holidays in Memphis. Again her parents balked. Again Elvis wheedled them into saying yes. After that visit Elvis decided he couldn't live without Priscilla. He managed to convince her parents to let her move to America and attend school in Memphis. Elvis told

Elvis was linked to a few actresses. One was
Ann-Margret, his costar in *Viva Las Vegas*.

Captain Beaulieu that Priscilla would live with Vernon and his new wife, Dee. In reality, she soon moved into Graceland with Elvis. She lived there while she earned her diploma at a Catholic high school.

Meanwhile, drug use was beginning to take a toll on Elvis. He took amphetamines to speed him up and to help him through the rigors of filming his movies and recording his albums. Then, struggling to sleep as he had for years, he took sleeping pills to slow down his body functions. It may have been the drugs. It may have been the pressure. But those around him saw his mood change. He had always had a hot temper, but now they witnessed violent mood swings. They noticed "not just the loss of control but the absence of remorse in a nature that each of them saw as essentially soft-hearted, for good or for ill," wrote biographer Guralnick.[13]

At the same time, Elvis also began to look for a deeper purpose in his life. His hairdresser, Larry Geller, talked to him for hours about spirituality. He provided Elvis with many books on the subject. He convinced Elvis that the purpose in life is to discover the purpose of life. "That's what we're born to do." That idea moved Elvis, who often wondered why he had been chosen to become a superstar.[14]

"Elvis was looking for meaning and Larry seemed to have some answers," Priscilla later recalled. "Or at least he understood Elvis's questions."[15]

Parker and members of the Memphis Mafia believed Geller was bad for Elvis. They thought Geller was trying to control Elvis's already fragile psyche. They thought Geller was making Elvis crazy. In the end, the Colonel banished

Geller from ever being alone with Elvis. Eventually, Geller dropped out of Elvis's life for several years.

The nature of pop stardom dictates that most artists remain popular for just a few years. Some fade, and others rise to replace them. By the mid-1960s it appeared that Elvis was beginning a slow, but steady slide. His songs no longer dominated the pop charts. His movies, while still popular, had lost some of their box office appeal.

In addition, he was beginning to lose some of his sex appeal. He had begun to put on weight. Growing up in poverty, Elvis did not have a wide choice of foods. When he became wealthy, he could have as much of whatever foods he wanted. The temptation proved more than he could handle.

> **By the mid-1960s it appeared that Elvis was beginning a slow, but steady slide.**

At Graceland, there was a cook on duty twenty-four hours a day ready to prepare a meal whenever Elvis might be hungry. Elvis ate often, and he usually ate large portions. He enjoyed fried food and food prepared in rich buttery sauces. Over the years, his poor eating habits took a toll on both his digestive system and his heart.

On the occasion of his thirtieth birthday in 1965, *Time* magazine called him "the grand-daddy of big-time rock 'n' roll." Even worse, the article pointed out that "his second-skin jeans have been replaced by somewhat wider slacks."[16]

After nearly a decade at the top, was Elvis mania finally waning? Elvis managed to find ways to ensure that this would not happen.

Chapter 10

Marriage, Birth, and Rebirth

Just when it appeared that Elvis Presley might be fading from the public consciousness, several things came together to put him firmly in the news again. In 1967, Elvis seemed to regain some of his momentum both personally and professionally.

In December 1966, he bought a horse for Priscilla Beaulieu as a Christmas present. He gave her another present as well: a three-and-a-half-carat diamond engagement ring. Elvis said, "I told you I'd know when the time was right. Well, the time's right."[1]

Like most of his interests, Elvis dove into the world of horses with wild enthusiasm. Soon he purchased a horse of his own. Then he bought horses for his entourage and their wives. "The happiest I ever saw him was when he developed a passion for horses," Priscilla said.[2]

In early 1967, he bought a horse farm in Mississippi not far from Memphis. He named it the Circle G (for Graceland). The one-hundred-sixty-acre property cost more than four hundred thousand dollars. He spent thousands more on horses and on bringing trailers to the property so that he and his entourage and their wives could live there. Soon, Elvis and his entourage adopted "the communal cowboy life." However, as with many of Elvis's passions, his interest in this one soon waned. He put the ranch up for sale less than a year after buying it.

Meanwhile, other aspects of his life and business were changing as well. A new "partnership agreement" with Colonel Tom Parker went into effect at the beginning of 1967. The arrangement gave Parker a 50 percent share in many aspects of Elvis's business.

Parker asked for this deal for several reasons. For one thing, he feared the unpredictability of Elvis's fame and the increasing unpredictability of Elvis himself. "If he was going to tie his future and devote all of his considerable energies to one performer, there was little question in his mind that he should be getting some equity, too," wrote Elvis biographer Peter Guralnick.[3]

In February 1967, RCA released Elvis's religious album *How Great Thou Art*. The album received much critical praise. Sales were slow at first, but the album sold steadily for many years. It also earned Elvis his first Grammy Award, winning the 1967 award for "Best Sacred Performance." Grammy Awards are the top honors in the recording industry.

This album again demonstrated Elvis's ability to perform across genres. It also allowed him to return to his musical roots, singing the gospel music he had enjoyed so much as a young child. The title hymn was one of Elvis's favorites, and "something special happened when Elvis sang this song." It "displayed the soul of Elvis, a part of himself he was eager to share."[4]

The King and His Queen

Then, on the morning of May 1, 1967, one of the most eligible bachelors in the world went off the market. That day Elvis married Priscilla in a suite at the Aladdin Hotel in Las Vegas. Colonel Parker made most of the arrangements. The ceremony itself was small and private. Only a handful of relatives and a couple of friends attended.

In fact, most of Elvis's entourage—his closest friends—were not even invited. Many of them took this snub hard. Red West even quit for two years. "The truth is, the suite the ceremony was in was big enough for the rest of the guys to be there," said Marty Lacker, who served as one of two best men for the wedding. "But the Colonel invited who he wanted."[5]

> On the morning of May 1, 1967, one of the most eligible bachelors in the world went off the market.

After the wedding, the bride and groom held a press conference as reporters peppered them with questions. "We appear calm," Elvis noted, "but Ed Sullivan didn't scare me this much."[6]

The newlyweds spent two days in Palm Springs, and then flew back to Memphis. Later that month, they donned their wedding attire again. They held a reception at Graceland for friends, relatives, and employees. Elvis wore a black suit. Priscilla wore a chiffon dress with a six-foot train. After the Graceland reception, Elvis and

Priscilla headed off to the Circle G Ranch, where they spent a peaceful honeymoon.

"Sadly, the peace was not long lived," Priscilla later recalled. "Forces he could not avoid—or chose not to avoid—were calling him back. His world would not remain calm."[7]

Indeed, his movie career continued slipping in 1967. Early in the year he filmed *Clambake*, one of his least favorites among all his movies. He complained to studio executives about the script, but no substantive improvements were made.

"Elvis was so despondent over *Clambake* that his weight ballooned from his usual 170 to 200 pounds by the time he reported for work," Priscilla later recalled. To get his weight back down, he resorted to diet pills.[8]

To make matters even worse, Elvis tripped in the bathroom the day he was to report for filming. He suffered a concussion, and production on the movie had to be delayed. Later he delayed filming once again for a more embarrassing reason. He had saddle sores from riding horses at his ranch.

For relief from his saddle sores, Elvis called Dr. George Nichopoulos to treat him at the ranch. The two hit it off, and "Dr. Nick" went on to treat the King's illnesses (and provide his prescription drugs) for the rest of Elvis's life. Although visitors to the ranch commented on how fit Elvis looked, in reality he was often under the influence of a variety of pills. Some days, according to a member of his entourage, he was so stoned that he could barely stay aboard his horse.[9]

Then something happened that caused Elvis to straighten out his life—at least for awhile. In July, as he worked on the movie *Speedway* with costar Nancy Sinatra, he announced to the press that Priscilla was pregnant. "This is the greatest thing that has ever happened to me," he said.[10]

Elvis Comes Back Strong

The year 1968 began well for Elvis. In January the Colonel finalized a deal with NBC for Elvis to do a Christmas special—his first television appearance since 1960. Between the appearance and the film that would be made from the performance footage, Elvis would earn more than one million dollars.

At 5:01 P.M. on February 1, 1968, Elvis became a father, as Priscilla gave birth to a baby girl. They named their daughter Lisa Marie. At first, family life seemed to suit Elvis. He continued to make movies, which meant that he spent much time away from Graceland. When home, however, he doted on his daughter. Priscilla and Lisa Marie also spent time at a home that Elvis had bought in Los Angeles in late 1967. That gave them a chance to spend more time together while Elvis filmed his movies.

> **Elvis became a father, as Priscilla gave birth to a baby girl.**

In May 1968, the family took a vacation to Hawaii. While there, Elvis and Priscilla attended Ed Parker's karate championship tournament. Karate was Elvis's favorite way of exercising and staying in shape. He eventually

Elvis and Priscilla with their daughter Lisa Marie in 1968.

earned a seventh-degree black belt. He even filmed a karate-based dance scene for his NBC special, but the scene was later cut.

Originally planned as strictly a Christmas special, Elvis's appearance on NBC later became an Elvis retrospective, with material spanning his career. The show revolved around the theme of a young man searching for happiness, with the song "Guitar Man" serving as a link to tie together the sequences. The idea of appearing live again energized Elvis, who spent about a month preparing for the show, which was taped at the end of June.

Elvis spent much of the summer filming a Western film called *Charro*. He enjoyed playing a dramatic role that was not built around singing. Still, as in so many of his movies, he was saddled with a mediocre script and rushed production schedule. *Variety* magazine summed it up by saying, "Elvis strolls through a role that would have driven any other actor up the wall."[11]

But if Elvis felt frustrated by his lightweight movie roles, he felt vindicated by reaction to the Elvis special. The show aired on December 3 and ranked as the number-one television show of the season. Parker had wanted Elvis to do a straight Christmas show. For once Elvis stood up to his mentor, and his instincts proved true.

Attired in a black leather outfit for parts of the show, Elvis looked like the Elvis of old. He had never sounded better. For this special, Elvis rocked. He crooned. He performed with the passion that had marked his rise to stardom in the 1950s. And the audience loved it.

Elvis admitted that the notion of taping in front of a live audience made him nervous. "For nearly ten years, I have been kept away from the public," he said. "And the one thing I loved was performing. But I'm not sure they're going to like me now."[12]

Elvis needn't have worried. Critics and fans alike loved his performance. The show became known as the "comeback special." It marked his reemergence as a force on the music scene. The show closed with the song "If I Can Dream," inspired by Martin Luther King, Jr.'s "I Have a Dream" speech. King had been assassinated in Memphis earlier in 1968. Elvis greatly admired King and had memorized King's famous speech.

In 1968, Elvis had a comeback. He looked and sounded like his old self.

Attired in a white suit and red tie, Elvis poured his heart and soul into performing this song, which offered a plea for peace and brotherhood. He closed with arms spread dramatically, and then uttered the words that impersonators have so often imitated: "Thank you. Thank you very much."[13]

Elvis's "comeback" continued to gather steam in January 1969. For his next album, he returned to Memphis, where he had recorded his first hits. One reason for his lackluster material during the 1960s rested with Parker's insistence that writers sign over a portion of the publishing rights for any song that Elvis recorded. Most top songwriters would not accept those terms. For this Memphis session, Elvis declared, "I don't care who owns it or what the deal is, I don't care about publishing, I don't care about writers, I just want some great material."[14]

The Memphis sessions yielded four strong singles. These included "Don't Cry Daddy" and "Kentucky Rain" as well as two songs that ranked as all-time Elvis classics: "In the Ghetto" and "Suspicious Minds." "In the Ghetto" was a topical song about a poor young urban male who gets caught up in a life of crime and ends up dying. It probably touched Elvis because it reminded him of his own poverty-stricken youth. The song reached number three.

"He was just really into it," recalled Reggie Young, who played guitar on the record. "I remember it being stopped a few times—he just wanted to do it better. It was like he was finally doing a song with some meaning to it, with some soul."[15]

"Suspicious Minds," meanwhile, became Elvis's first number-one hit in seven years. The song cemented the King's comeback, and it remained one of his favorite songs to perform in concert throughout the rest of his career.

"An eternal tale of paranoia and deceit, it evidently struck a chord with Elvis, who heightened the tension of the verses and then poured out his heart," added John Robertson. "With the female backing singers urging him on, Elvis took the song . . . to its brooding climax."[16]

The Memphis recording sessions also yielded the tracks for two albums: *From Elvis in Memphis* and *Back in Memphis*. The former is a true classic that *The Rolling*

Stone Album Guide calls "one of the finest studio albums of his career."[17]

Back in Memphis is strong as well. Biographer Guralnick said that the personal resonance Elvis found in some of these songs announced "the birth of a new hybrid style, a cross between 'Old Shep' and contemporary soul, in which Elvis can fully believe."[18]

> **"Suspicious Minds," meanwhile, became Elvis's first number-one hit in seven years.**

Amazingly, some fifteen years after bursting onto the scene, Elvis had reinvented himself through his television special and his latest recordings. Moreover, he had finally completed his commitment to the grind of making movies. In his last film, *Change of Habit*, he played a doctor working in the slums of New York with a nun played by Mary Tyler Moore.

A Lavish Show in Las Vegas

His last film was not bad, but he felt relieved to be done making them. The success of his television special and his latest recording sessions rekindled his passion for music. He decided that he wanted to return to singing live. With that in mind, the Colonel booked him to perform for four weeks at the brand-new International Hotel in Las Vegas.

The stage show Elvis put on was elaborate and lavish. He wanted to embrace all the types of music he had loved over the years. He assembled a cast of talented background singers and musicians, and he rehearsed diligently.

At 10:15 P.M. on opening night, August 1, 1969, the sellout crowd of two thousand rose to its feet and roared as Elvis strode onstage. Wearing a modified black karate suit, tied at the waist and open down the front, Elvis appeared as sexy and appealing as ever as he sang and moved. He was described as "bursting with energy, falling to his knees, sliding across the stage, even doing somersaults."[19]

The invitation-only crowd, which included many celebrities and reporters, remained standing and cheering through most of the show. Highlights included a six-minute version of "Suspicious Minds" and his encore song, "Can't Help Falling in Love."

The audience loved the show. Critics did, too. David Dalton of *Rolling Stone* said, "Elvis was supernatural, his own resurrection." "There are several unbelievable things about Elvis," said *Newsweek*, "but the most incredible is his staying power in a world where meteoric careers fade like shooting stars."[20]

Within hours after the performance, the Colonel met with the hotel management to revise and extend the contract. Elvis was to receive one hundred twenty-five thousand dollars a week for two four-week engagements a year through 1974. This came to one million a year for just eight weeks work, although Elvis had to pay for all of the show expenses out of this.

Amazingly, the decade of the 1960s ended just as it began—with Elvis Presley standing as the King of Rock 'n' Roll. Furthermore, he appeared poised to extend his reign into the 1970s as well. Sadly, it was not to be.

Chapter 11

Caught in a Trap

In "Suspicious Minds," Elvis Presley sang about being "caught in a trap." In many ways, that summed up his life as the 1970s began. At first glance, everything seemed great. Elvis rode a huge wave of popularity, and his latest records were hits. His performances in Las Vegas had drawn rave reviews. Once again the King reigned upon his throne.

In some ways, however, Elvis still faced many of the same challenges and dangers that had dragged down his career during much of the 1960s. In deciding to tour again, he simply replaced the rigorous schedule of moviemaking with a series of energy-draining tour stops. And to cope with those rigors, he once again turned to drugs—amphetamines to help him get up for performances, sleeping pills to help him wind down, and diet pills to help keep off weight.

In February 1970, Elvis made four historic appearances at the Houston Astrodome as part of the

Houston Livestock Show and Rodeo. After one rehearsal in the cavernous stadium, which seated around forty-five thousand people, Elvis realized that the acoustics were terrible. "This is gonna be rather atrocious," he told the other musicians, "so don't fight it, go ahead and play."[1]

At the first show, he was discouraged not only by the poor acoustics, but also by what he deemed to be a luke-warm reaction from a less-than-capacity crowd. By the second show, however, both he and the audience had regained their enthusiasm. At the evening show on the second day, 43,614 fans attended. He also expressed pleasure at the response from the media critics. Robert Hilburn of the *Los Angeles Times* described the perform-ance as "masterful."[2]

In April, his song "The Wonder of You" was released, reaching number nine on the charts. In June, Elvis spent several days recording in Nashville. He ended up focusing on country and-western songs. Some of these songs later formed the basis for the album *Elvis Country*.

August found Elvis back in Las Vegas. Once again audiences went wild at the sold-out shows. During this engagement he turned his habit of handing out scarves to fans into a central part of the show. He also mixed in plenty of banter and jokes. Footage from these perform-ances formed the basis for the documentary film *That's the Way It Is*.

In early September, Elvis embarked on a brief tour—his first since 1957. It went so well that another tour immediately followed. Colonel Tom Parker saw touring as a surefire way to generate income—lots of income.

In 1970, Elvis starred in a documentary called *That's the Way It Is*.

Heartache and Death Threats

Elvis's hectic schedule took its toll on his family life. When Elvis Presley first began doing his Las Vegas engagements, Priscilla and Lisa Marie visited frequently. When they were apart, Priscilla sent Elvis daily "care packages" of photos and tape recordings of his little girl.

Over time, however, Priscilla found that Elvis's renewed popularity began to drive a wedge between them. "Thriving on all the excitement, glamour, and hysteria, he found it difficult to go home and resume his role as father and husband," she later wrote. "And for me the impossibility of replacing the crowd's adoration became a real-life nightmare."[3]

Priscilla bristled at the continuing rumors of Elvis's affairs with other women. In 1970, a woman named

Priscilla found that Elvis's renewed popularity began to drive a wedge between them.

Patricia Parker filed a paternity suit against Elvis, claiming he had fathered her child. Blood tests proved that he was not the father, but Priscilla realized that his sexual behavior made it possible for such a claim to be true. In November 1970, Elvis admitted to the press that his marriage was "going through a difficult patch."[4]

Elvis also endured a number of death threats, including one that involved blackmail. An anonymous person demanded to be paid fifty thousand dollars to reveal the name of the person who intended to kill Elvis. Elvis also received a copy of the hotel menu, which had a picture of him on the front. The person had drawn a gun pointing at his head. Both Elvis and the Federal Bureau of Investigation (FBI) took such threats seriously. Extra security was added, and Elvis carried a derringer— a type of small pistol—in his boot.

Elvis had collected guns for years. He often carried them with him when he traveled. His collection included gold-plated pistols and two other guns that he had had jewelers decorate with gold. He bought guns for members of his entourage as well. In the 1970s, his collection numbered thirty-eight weapons, including an assault rifle and a submachine gun.

Meeting the President

Elvis's fixation with guns led to one of his more interesting outings in 1970. In December, following an argument with Vernon Presley and Priscilla over expenses

Elvis met with President Nixon in 1970.

(including twenty thousand dollars for guns) he flew to Washington, D.C., on a whim. Once there, he sought a meeting with President Richard Nixon.

Elvis had an interesting reason for wanting to meet the president. He wanted Nixon to give him a federal narcotics officer's badge. Although not an Elvis fan, Nixon agreed to meet the singer. It was an odd meeting indeed—the conservative Nixon in a suit and Elvis in his open shirt and gold jewelry.

Elvis offered to help Nixon in the war against illegal drugs in the United States. He thought that as a celebrity he might be able to help deliver an antidrug message to young people. This may seem ironic in light of Elvis's own dependence on pills. Elvis, however, did not consider his pills "drugs." To him, they were all prescribed medications, which put them into an entirely different category.

In the end, Elvis was designated a "special assistant" in the Bureau of Narcotics and Dangerous Drugs (BNDD), receiving both a badge and a photo identification card from the U.S. Department of Justice. Although Elvis received an official badge, the BNDD did not intend him to be involved in the bureau's work in any real way. Still, wrote Adam Victor, "Elvis believed that this badge gave him the authority to carry guns and whatever pharmaceuticals he wanted anywhere in the country."[5]

Living Legend

Soon after, Elvis received another significant honor. The Junior Chambers of Commerce (Jaycees) named him one of their outstanding young men in the nation for 1970. Meanwhile, Elvis continued to play to record audiences during his engagements in Las Vegas and a separate engagement in Lake Tahoe in 1971. His standard ensemble for performing now featured sequined jumpsuits.

Still in the prime of his career, Elvis had already become a living legend. In June 1971 the two-room house in Tupelo, Mississippi, in which he was born opened for tours to the public. Around the same time, a long stretch of Highway 51 South, part of which runs in front of Graceland, was officially renamed Elvis Presley Boulevard.

In the summer of 1971, Elvis received the Bing Crosby Award from the National Academy of Recording Arts and Sciences. This special recognition is given for lifetime achievement, and Elvis received it at the age of thirty-six.

Elvis capped his professional year with a successful tour of a dozen cities in the fall. His outfits grew more elaborate, his glittery black or white jumpsuit now accompanied by a matching cape. Fans loved the glitz, the glamour, and hearing Elvis's golden voice.

> **Still in the prime of his career, Elvis had already become a living legend.**

The Queen Moves Out

All of these accomplishments, however, were overshadowed by the disintegration of Elvis's marriage in 1971. His constant inattention and womanizing finally grew too much for Priscilla to endure.

Ironically, karate played a role in the breakup. Priscilla started her training so that she and Elvis would have an activity to share. As his schedule kept him away more and more often, she continued training, first with kung fu expert Ed Parker and later with karate expert Mike Stone. The training increased her self-confidence and lessened her dependence on Elvis. She longed for a more normal life.

Also, Priscilla found herself falling in love with Stone. She realized that with him she could enjoy all of the simple pleasures that life with Elvis could never offer. When Priscilla told Elvis she was leaving, he asked if he had lost her to another man. "It's not that you've lost me to another man," she replied. "You've lost me to a life of my own. I'm finding myself for the first time."[6]

115

Priscilla and Lisa Marie left Graceland on December 30, 1971. They flew back to California to live. Elvis's friend Jerry Schilling recalls that after they left, Elvis shut himself in his bedroom. "Once I heard him cursing, another time screaming but mostly sobbing," Schilling said. "That was the beginning of the end for the Elvis I had known and loved."[7]

Burning Up the Charts

At first Elvis kept moving forward as if nothing had happened. In 1972, Elvis continued to perform in Las Vegas and Lake Tahoe. In March and April, MGM filmed Elvis in a recording and on tour. The resulting film, *Elvis on Tour*, won a Golden Globe award for Best Documentary. In April, he released a gospel album titled *He Touched Me*. That album went on to win a Grammy Award for Best Inspirational Performance.

> **Priscilla and Lisa Marie left Graceland on December 30, 1971.**

In June 1972, Elvis performed at four sold-out shows at New York's famed Madison Square Garden. The star-studded audience went wild, and *Time* magazine hailed his comeback as "perhaps the most impressive in the history of pop music."[8]

Meanwhile, Elvis's latest single, "Burning Love," was just about to burn up the airwaves. This energetic song was the first true rock-and-roll song he had released in some time, and it captured some of the old magic of his early days in music. Ironically, wrote Paul Simpson, "Elvis didn't want to record 'Burning Love,' didn't like it when he had recorded it, and sang it as rarely as possible afterwards."[9]

His fans, however, felt differently, propelling the song to number two on the Billboard charts. "Built around a tense rhythm that was always on the verge of bubbling over, 'Burning Love' reminded the world why Elvis had been called the King of Rock 'n' Roll," wrote John Robertson.[10]

"Burning Love" proved to be Elvis's last top-ten single. However, Elvis continued to place songs on the country charts during the 1970s. Over his career, he recorded hits that spanned from rock to country, from rhythm and blues to gospel. His versatility and longevity stand as hallmarks of his career.

Following his split with Priscilla, Elvis had a steady stream of women. Then in July 1972, he met Memphis State University student Linda Thompson, the reigning Miss Tennessee. They began a four-and-a-half-year relationship. Seemingly bolstered by his new romance, Elvis dove into preparations for another historic event— a live show that would be beamed by satellite all over the world. For years, Elvis had wanted to do a world tour. Colonel Parker had always found excuses to keep this from happening. Parker offered the satellite event as an alternative.

On January 14, 1973, more than one billion people worldwide watched live as Elvis performed in Honolulu, Hawaii. *Aloha From Hawaii* drew the highest-ever share of the television audience in Japan, and an amazing 92 percent of viewers in the Philippines. In the United States, viewers didn't see the concert until April. "This is Elvis at his most iconic," said one review, "the Elvis his impersonators would aspire to become."[11]

Soon after, the soundtrack album for the special was released, and it rose to number one on the Billboard chart. It remained there for a full year.

On March 1, Parker arranged for the sale of Elvis's back catalog of songs to RCA. For a one-time payment of $5.4 million, RCA purchased the rights to all material recorded before 1973, with no further royalties to Elvis and Parker. At the same time, Elvis entered into a new management agreement with Parker. The deal provided a fifty-fifty split of all income except touring. Elvis also signed a new seven-year contract with the record company. In all, approximately $10.5 million changed hands in these transactions. Because of the way the deals were structured, Parker received approximately $6 million and Elvis $4.5 million.

A Downward Spiral

Soon after Elvis's triumphant satellite performance, however, things began to go wrong. Bored by the routine of performing in Las Vegas, Elvis began to put on weight. His use of pills increased. At one point, he had to cancel five performances because of ill health. Although audiences still enjoyed his shows, the critics blasted Elvis. "The Living Legend is fat and ludicrously aping his former self," wrote the *Hollywood Reporter*.[12]

Then Priscilla, concerned about Elvis's drug use, suggested that Lisa Marie not see him for awhile. Elvis flew into a rage. Blaming Stone, Priscilla's boyfriend, Elvis actually threatened to have Stone killed. Eventually, however, he calmed down.

In September, Elvis got into a bitter argument with Colonel Parker. During one of his Las Vegas shows, Elvis complained about the fact that the Hilton Hotel—who was paying him to perform—treated one of his favorite employees poorly. Parker yelled at Elvis for being "unprofessional." Elvis then fired his long-time manager. That lasted until the Colonel presented a detailed accounting of money he claimed Elvis owed him. In the end, Elvis backed down.

The divorce between Elvis and Priscilla became final on October 9, 1973. The split was, for the most part, amicable. The agreement called for joint custody of Lisa Marie, and she continued to visit Elvis regularly. Elvis spoiled Lisa Marie, buying her a pony and her own golf cart to ride around Graceland. "I saw her as a little Elvis," her Aunt Patsy later recalled. "She was ornery, outspoken, and a natural-born rebel."[13]

Just a week after the divorce, Elvis went into a Memphis hospital due to breathing problems. He remained there for more than two weeks. Doctors identified several problems, including his dependence on prescription drugs. Even some of his closest friends began to express concern about his growing drug use.

In early 1974, Elvis performed a series of shows in Memphis. These marked his first live appearances in his hometown since 1961. He continued to do his Las Vegas shows and tour across the country, but the quality of his performances from show to show varied widely.

Life's book *Remembering Elvis: 30 Years Later* said this about Elvis's concerts in those days: "Attending an Elvis concert in the '70s was like rolling the dice in a Vegas casino: anything from a jackpot to a crap-out was possible. His jumpsuits were spectacular—but if his weight was out of control, he was liable to bust his seams, as he did one night in Pontiac, Mich., before 62,000 astonished fans."[14]

> **Just a week after the divorce, Elvis went into a Memphis hospital due to breathing problems.**

On other occasions, he rambled in lengthy monologues or forgot the lyrics to songs. Elvis had been changing lyrics to certain songs for years. But now it appeared to many observers that these lapses were accidental rather than on purpose.

In April 1975 came an offer that almost rescued Elvis from his doldrums. Actress Barbra Streisand's production company offered Elvis a role in her forthcoming movie *A Star Is Born*. The movie, which depicts a classic Hollywood tale of success and failure, would provide a perfect vehicle for Elvis to revive his film career. Furthermore, the role seemed tailor-made for him. The deal fell through when Parker demanded a higher salary than the producers were willing to offer.

Later in April, Elvis bought a used Convair 880 jet at a cost of two hundred fifty thousand dollars. He renamed it the *Lisa Marie* and spent an additional half million dollars refurbishing it. For instance, he installed a queen-sized bed, gold plumbing fixtures, and a videotape system.

Throughout the rest of 1975 and 1976, Elvis continued to tour and perform, with his performances becoming increasingly erratic. He spent money wildly. In a single week in August 1975, he bought Parker an airplane (which Parker declined to accept), he spent one hundred forty thousand dollars on fourteen Cadillacs, and he gave Dr. Nick an interest-free loan of two hundred thousand dollars to build a new home.[15]

The year 1976 also was marked by both personal and personnel problems. On the personnel side, friction mounted with Sonny West and Red West. The two bodyguards had caused several lawsuits to be brought against Elvis after they used excessive force in dealing with unruly fans. In July, Vernon fired them, along with Dave Hebler, in what he termed a cost-cutting measure.

Deeply offended by this treatment, the Wests and Hebler began preparing a tell-all book titled *Elvis: What Happened?* (told to writer Steve Dunleavy), which detailed Elvis's drug use and other erratic behavior. Elvis tried to make amends with his former friends, but it was too late.

In October 1976, Linda Thompson left as well. She could no longer handle the constant attention and pampering that Elvis required. "He needed and wanted more love than anyone I've ever met," she said.[16]

Although Elvis immediately found another girlfriend, nineteen-year-old Ginger Alden, it was clear that his support system was falling apart. Still, he rallied to give a spirited New Year's performance in Pittsburgh, Pennsylvania. There appeared to be hope that he might still be able to turn things around.

Chapter 12

The King Is Dead

Unfortunately, that hope proved short lived. In January 1977, Elvis Presley failed even to show up for a scheduled recording session in Nashville. An article in the *Nashville Banner* suggested that Elvis is "paranoid and . . . afraid to record."[1]

He tried to rouse his spirits by proposing to Ginger Alden. He gave her a ring featuring the eleven-and-a-half-carat diamond out of his own Taking Care of Business (TCB) ring. The two did not set a wedding date.

Colonel Tom Parker, panicking after Elvis missed his recording session, brought Dr. Nick in to keep a close eye on Elvis's drug intake. He even allowed Larry Geller to come back in hopes that it would raise Elvis's spirits. Geller, who had not seen Elvis in some time, was appalled. "No one saw the hard fact that Elvis was on a track toward death," he later wrote. "No one wanted to see it. They were just blind, and in denial. Everybody was in denial."[2]

Elvis did one brief tour in February and another in March. On March 30, he stumbled through songs and sounded weary. He even forgot (or purposely changed) the lyrics to his classic song "Can't Help Falling in Love" from "Wise men say/Only fools rush in" to "Wise men know/When it's time to go." Was it an accident, or was Elvis foreseeing an end to his career?[3]

On March 31, 1977, Elvis grew so ill that he had to cancel the final few dates of his tour. That day, too, he learned from the tell-all book by Red West, Sonny West, and Dave Hebler was coming out that summer. Elvis feared the book would show only one aspect of his life and portray him in the worst possible light.

Elvis worried how his fans would react to revelations about his drug use and behavior with women. He hoped fans would see the book as an attempt to discredit him and pay little attention to its claims. He was even more concerned about what his father and daughter would think.

When he got home from his tour at the beginning of April, Elvis checked into a hospital in Memphis. In just a few days, he was discharged, and he went home to Graceland.

"A Parody of Himself"

Within three weeks, however, he began yet another tour. To keep him company, he brought along his girlfriend, Ginger. The tour was disastrous. Comments from reviewers and fans included such notes as "seeming not to care" and "he stunk."[4]

> **Elvis feared the book would show only one aspect of his life and portray him in the worst possible light.**

A writer in Detroit summed it up this way: "At best, he is a parody of himself. . . . It was a merciful gesture when Presley left the stage following his brief and disappointing performance and refused to make a curtain call."[5]

On May 29, 1977, at a performance in Baltimore, Elvis had to leave the stage to his backup singers for half an hour. He came back and simply said, "When you gotta go, you gotta go."[6]

Shows in Omaha, Nebraska, and Rapid City, South Dakota, were being filmed for an upcoming television special. Concerned about his weight and how he would look on-screen, Elvis took diet pills on top of the pain pills, amphetamines, and sleeping pills he already took. The performance in Omaha was a disaster, but he rallied for the show in Rapid City. "He looked healthier, seemed to have lost a little weight, and sounded better, too," wrote biographer Peter Guralnick.[7]

When that tour ended, Elvis went home to Graceland. He tried to relax, but as the publication date for the book that his former entourage members had written drew closer, he grew increasingly worried about how the book would affect his already declining career. He had even more trouble than usual sleeping.

The King's Last Days

Lisa Marie Presley arrived on July 31 for a visit. As always, Elvis spoiled her. He also rented out Libertyland, a local theme park, after hours one evening. The group of about twenty stayed all night. "His friends remember him as a proud father, somewhat solemn but fun loving as he accompanied her from ride to ride with the other children and adults he had invited to go with him," wrote biographer Jerry Hopkins.[8]

Elvis planned to depart on August 16 for a brief, ten-city tour that was scheduled to begin in Portland, Maine, the following day. At 10:30 P.M. on August 15, Elvis had a dentist's appointment with Dr. Hofman, who cleaned his teeth and filled a couple of small cavities. Elvis returned to Graceland shortly after midnight and went directly upstairs.

That night Elvis and Ginger talked about the upcoming tour. He wanted her to accompany him, but she preferred to come join him in a few days. They talked about marriage, and Elvis even said he might announce it at the Memphis concert at the end of the tour.

At 2:15 A.M. on August 16, Elvis called Dr. Nick and said that one of his new fillings was bothering him. Dr. Nick prescribed some pain medication, and a member of Elvis's entourage picked up the pills at an all-night pharmacy. A couple of hours later, Elvis called his cousin Billy Smith to play some racquetball. They played for only a few minutes before Elvis grew tired. He went back into the house and sang at the piano for a few minutes before going back upstairs.

Soon after that, he took the first of three packets of prescription drugs that he used each night to help him sleep. A couple of hours later he was still awake, so he took the second packet. Later he took the third and told Ginger he was going into the bathroom to read.

Ginger awoke around 1:30 P.M. on August 16 and saw that Elvis was not in bed. Soon after, she opened the bathroom door and found him lying on the floor. His face lay in a pool of vomit on the thick shag carpet. She immediately called for help. Members of Elvis's entourage rushed upstairs, but they soon realized there was nothing they could do.

Meanwhile, young Lisa Marie came to the bathroom door and saw her father on the floor. A few moments later, a man arrived at the front door to pick her up. She was scheduled to fly back to Los Angeles that day to rejoin her mother. "Sam!" she cried. "Sam! My daddy's dead! My daddy's dead!"[9]

An ambulance rushed Elvis to Baptist Memorial Hospital in Memphis. Efforts to revive him continued, but at 3:30 P.M., he was pronounced dead. An autopsy began at 7:00 P.M., but even before it was completed, the press was informed that Elvis died of "cardiac arrhythmia due to undertermined heartbeat." In other words, he had had a heart attack.[10]

> **Young Lisa Marie came to the bathroom door and saw her father on the floor.**

The results of the autopsy remained private. This led to rumors about his death that have lasted for years. Many people believed he died of a drug overdose. Some even thought he had committed suicide. A few, bizarrely, believed that he faked his death and remained alive.

Lab reports filed two months later described fourteen different drugs in Elvis's system at the time of his death.

Ten were present in significant quantities. Together, they could easily have caused a lethal overdose. Pharmacy records show that on the day before he died, Elvis received hundreds of pills, probably for the tour ahead. Controversy over his death raged for years.

Meanwhile, members of Elvis's entourage had the unpleasant duty of informing Priscilla, Vernon, and Colonel Parker that Elvis had died. Parker then had to handle all the details of canceling the tour, which was scheduled to begin the next day.

Graceland, as one of the emergency medical technicians described it, "was filled with hysteria." Vernon and Ginger seemed to be in shock, and Lisa Marie ran through the house crying, "My daddy is gone!"[11]

Meanwhile, a crowd of reporters had gathered at the hospital. Two of Elvis's friends tried but failed to break the news. They were too choked up. Finally, hospital administrator Maurice Elliott was given the job. "There were all sorts of TV cameras and radio microphones, and the room was just packed with people," he later recalled. He was stunned to think that "here I am in front of the world, and I am going to have to announce Elvis Presley's death."[12]

The World Mourns

News of Elvis's death spread quickly. Within hours, hundreds of mourners had gathered at Graceland. By the next day, their numbers had swelled to an estimated fifty thousand. From 3:00 to 6:30 P.M., mourners filed by the copper coffin, paying their tribute to the King.

Elvis's death was one that many people remembered. The hearse carrying Elvis's body leaves Graceland, August 18, 1977.

People came from all over the United States. Priscilla flew in from California to mourn her former husband and comfort her daughter.

Even many years later, people often remember exactly what they were doing when they hear monumental or tragic news. Thus it was with Elvis's death. Within hours, people heard the news on television or radio. Many remembered their experiences listening to Elvis's music. They mourned that he would never sing again.

Meanwhile, newspaper headlines across the world proclaimed his death. In Russia, a newspaper ran a full-page about Elvis's death. It simply said, "Elvis is dead.

The USA has given us three cultural phenomenon: Mickey Mouse, Coke a Cola (sic), and Elvis Presley." In France, the headline read: "L'Adieu a Elvis!" and in Britain the front page read, "King Elvis Dead at 42 and Alone."[13]

Even in death, Elvis was surrounded by a media circus. On August 18, a brief service was held at Graceland. The Reverend C. W. Bradley from a nearby Church of Christ gave the eulogy, saying: "Elvis was a frail human being. And he would be the first to admit his weaknesses. . . . Elvis would not want anyone to think that he had no flaws

The King was dead.

or faults. But now that he's gone, I find it more helpful to remember his good qualities, and I hope you do, too."[14]

Then the body was carried to Forest Hill Cemetery in a white hearse, followed by seventeen white limousines. A brief ceremony followed. Then Elvis was laid in a white marble mausoleum, near where his mother was buried. The next day, an estimated fifty thousand fans visited the cemetery, each taking home a single flower at the wish of the Presley family. Within two months, however, both Elvis and Gladys were reburied at Graceland.

The King was dead. But his memory and music lived on, sometimes in ways he might never have imagined.

Chapter 13

Long Live the King

Elvis Presley may be gone, but he lives on through his music and movies. Even today the public remains fascinated with him.

In death, as in life, Elvis remains big business. Long after his death, Elvis continues to generate huge amounts of income, bringing in an average of $45 million per year. This makes him the top-grossing dead celebrity, according to *Forbes* magazine. The income comes from Graceland visitors, CDs, and DVDs.[1]

Indeed, Elvis's death touched off a struggle for control of the Elvis empire. Colonel Tom Parker, as before, remained in control of much of the action. "Elvis didn't die," he said. "The body did. We're keeping up the good spirits. . . . I talked to him this morning, and he told me to carry on."[2]

Elvis's will named his father as executor and trustee of his will. Beneficiaries were his grandmother, Minnie Mae Presley, who still lived at Graceland, his father, and

Lisa Marie Presley. Vernon Presley left most of his affairs in the hands of Parker.

When Vernon died of a heart attack in 1979, control of Elvis's estate passed to Priscilla. She broke off from Parker, and a judge ordered an investigation of how Parker had managed his estate. In 1981, the court ordered that no further payments should be made to Parker, and in 1983, the Presley estate won a court action against the Colonel. The matter was settled out of court. The court-appointed attorney pointed out in his reports "that the several agreements he [Parker] entered into with RCA and others . . . could not—ever—have been in Elvis' best interests."[3]

Graceland opened on May 4, 1982.

The Colonel died in 1997 of a stroke. Of the estimated $100 million he earned managing Elvis, only $1 million remained in his estate when he died.

When Priscilla inherited Graceland, it appeared that she might have to sell it. It simply cost too much to keep it running. Still, Priscilla did not want to sell Graceland and its Elvis artifacts. She didn't want Lisa to "grow up and have regrets that everything had been sold."[4]

Then someone suggested that Graceland be opened to the public. Graceland opened on May 4, 1982. Priscilla was on hand to greet some three thousand guests who each paid five dollars to see where the King had lived. "Elvis was very proud of his home, and any time guests would come in he was more than willing to show them through the house," Priscilla said. "I think he'd be very pleased to know that the house is shown in this way."[5]

Priscilla Presley opened Graceland to visitors in 1982. People can tour the first floor of the house and walk by the graves of Elvis and his family.

Only the first floor of Graceland is open to the public. This includes the music room, the dining room, the TV room, the billiard room, the kitchen, and the den, which is also named the "jungle room" because of its décor. The Hall of Gold in Elvis's trophy building is lined with his gold and platinum albums. The hall pays tribute to his sales of more than one billion records worldwide, more than any other entertainer in history.[6]

Each year, more than six hundred thousand people visit Graceland, making it one of America's top five most-visited historic homes.

Some people come twice a year. They visit in January for Elvis's birthday and in August around the anniversary of his death. "Why all of us want to know so much about this one man is still a mystery to me," said Nancie Craft, president of an Elvis Presley fan club. "But we go because it's like a family reunion, and we all just feel closer to Elvis at Graceland."[7]

Meanwhile, Elvis's memory is kept alive by a seemingly never-ending string of books about various aspects of his life. Straight biographies, books focusing on his music, tales recounting scandals in his life, a day-by-day record of his life, and even *The Elvis Encyclopedia* cover everything about the King. Elvis has even become the topic of university courses on American culture.

Separate sets of books covered Colonel Parker, the Memphis Mafia, Priscilla, and Lisa Marie. Indeed, Priscilla and Lisa Marie went on to have careers of their own and to achieve some measure of fame in their own right. Priscilla starred in several movies, including three editions of the *Naked Gun* series of movies and several other films. She also had roles in a number of television programs. Most notable was her portrayal of Jenna Wade in the blockbuster television series *Dallas* in the 1980s. In 1992, she was cited by *People* magazine as one of the fifty most beautiful people in the world.

In addition, Priscilla served as executive producer for several television specials relating to Elvis's life. She also wrote the book *Elvis and Me*.

Lisa Marie followed in her father's footsteps by launching a career as a recording artist. She released the popular album *To Whom It May Concern* in 2003; other albums include *Now What*. Lisa Marie expressed pride at establishing her own reputation as a singer. "I got these fans through my music!" she said.[8]

However, Lisa Marie is probably best known for her brief marriage to another famous singer—Michael Jackson. The two were married from 1994 to 1996. During much of the 1980s, Jackson ranked as the most popular singer in the world. Known as the "King of Pop," Jackson had in some ways taken over the spot Elvis had held for so long.

By the 1990s, however, Jackson's career had begun to lag, just as Elvis's had done in the 1970s. Furthermore, Jackson had been accused of inappropriate behavior with young boys. Some people believed that Jackson's marriage to Lisa Marie was a sham. They thought he married her just to improve his public image.

In an interview with Oprah Winfrey in 2005, Lisa Marie said the marriage was real and that she truly loved him. However, when Oprah asked if Jackson had used her, Lisa Marie answered, "All signs point to yes on that."[9]

Lisa Marie made headlines again after having twin girls in late 2008 at age forty. "I really wanted these babies," Lisa Marie told *People* magazine. She added that she had been trying to get pregnant with husband Michael Lockwood for two years and that she had had several previous miscarriages.[10]

Not only do members of Elvis's family remain in the public eye, but so does Elvis himself. More than thirty years after his death, literally hundreds of fan clubs in dozens of countries also keep his memory alive. According to *The Elvis Encyclopedia*, "Fan club festivals continue around the world, not just in Memphis and Tupelo but also from Canada to Australia."[11]

People can see "Elvis" perform live even today. Elvis impersonators (or Elvis tribute artists, as they prefer to

Las Vegas is home to many Elvis impersonators. This couple was just married by "Elvis."

be called) perform throughout Las Vegas and across the United States. There is even a Professional Elvis Impersonators Association with members from across the United States, Canada, and Japan.

But, most of all, Elvis lives on through his music. Somewhere in the world at any moment of the day or night, it is almost certain that an Elvis song is playing on someone's music system or on some radio station. In fact, Sirius Satellite Radio established Elvis Radio, which bills itself as "the only all Elvis all-the-time radio station, broadcasting live from Graceland."

Elvis's songs and his influence have stood the test of time. According to *Livewire*, Elvis Presley ranks number seven on the list of top ten most influential rock artists of all time. Although other people wrote his words and music,

Elvis lives on through his music.

Livewire noted that "with a delivery and performance so potent that his lower body had to be censored from television viewers it made absolutely no difference."[12]

In 1986, Elvis was among the first inductees into the Rock and Roll Hall of Fame in Cleveland, Ohio. In 1992, his image appeared on a U.S. postage stamp.

The Elvis legacy lives on through all the other artists he has influenced. These include the Rolling Stones, Led Zeppelin, and Bob Dylan, noted *Livewire*.

Fellow Rock and Roll Hall of Fame member Bruce Springsteen once hopped the fence at Graceland in hopes of meeting his idol. Elvis was not home, and his security guards escorted Springsteen back out to the street. Springsteen further recalled that after watching Elvis perform on *The Ed Sullivan Show*, "I had to get a guitar the next day." An unhappy loner growing up, Springsteen claimed that "his life was saved by rock 'n' roll."[13]

The Beatles credit Elvis with being a major influence on them. John Lennon said that "Heartbreak Hotel" was "the most exciting thing [we'd] ever heard. It was the spark, and then the whole world opened up for us."[14]

A closer analysis of "Heartbreak Hotel" may illuminate Elvis's career as well as anything. Elvis was still considered primarily a rockabilly singer and had only a regional following when he recorded this song written by Mae Boren Axton and Tommy Durden.

According to Fred Bronson, Durden brought Axton a newspaper story about a suicide victim who had left a one-line note saying, "I walk a lonely street." Axton came up with the idea of adding a "heartbreak hotel" at the end of that street. When she played a demo for Elvis, "he asked to hear it again—and again—until he had listened to it 10 times," said Bronson.[15] He found the song fascinating.

RCA, Elvis's new record label, was much less enthused. "Heartbreak Hotel" marked Elvis's first single after signing with RCA, and record executives were not convinced the song would be a hit. Somber and almost ghoulish in nature, the song hardly seemed a top-forty candidate. Elvis's instincts proved correct. "Heartbreak Hotel" went on to sell 2 million copies and became his first national number one hit.

Elvis's songs and his influence have stood the test of time.

According to Toby Creswell, "The reverb that dominates the sound of the track was created by putting a speaker at the end of a hallway." Together the musical effect and Elvis's distinctive voice created a unique sound that still reverberates more than fifty years later.[16]

In many ways, "Heartbreak Hotel" typifies Elvis's early career. He chose excellent songs and delivered them with a styling that marked the songs as his own. Over time, he conquered the worlds of rock and roll, country music, rhythm and blues, and gospel. He became the world's biggest pop icon, so well known that he needed only a single name—Elvis.

Yes, Elvis changed the face of American pop culture. He paved the way for the superstar musicians who followed. He was, and always will be, truly the King.

Chronology

1935—Elvis Aaron Presley is born on January 8 in Tupelo, Mississippi; his twin brother, Jesse Garon, is born dead.

1936—A tornado tears through Tupelo, killing more than two hundred people, it destroys the church across the street from the Presleys, but leaves their house untouched.

1937—Elvis's father, Vernon, is sent to prison for illegally altering the amount on a check.

1940—The Presley family briefly moves to Pascagoula, Mississippi; they stay only a few months.

1941—Elvis starts first grade in 1941; the United States enters World War II in December following the Japanese attack on the U.S. naval base at Pearl Harbor, Hawaii.

1945—Sings at a talent show at the annual Mississippi-Alabama Fair and Dairy Show, winning fifth place.

1946—Gets his first guitar and soon begins taking it to school.

1948—The Presley family moves to Memphis, Tennessee.

1949—Enters Humes High School and stands out because of his long, slicked-back hair and colorful clothing.

1953—Wins the senior class variety show with his singing; graduates from high school on June 3, the first member of his immediate family to earn a diploma; pays four dollars to record two songs to give to his mother as a present.

1954—Begins dating Dixie Locke; called in to Sun Studio to record; releases his first record, "That's All Right," which becomes a hit; performs his first concert.

1955—Begins touring; becomes a regular at the popular *Louisiana Hayride*; signs with RCA records after RCA buys his contract from Sun.

1956—Breaks through on the national scene with four number-one hit records, including the classics "Heartbreak Hotel" and "Hound Dog"; signs management contract with Colonel Tom Parker; performs on several national television shows, including *The Ed Sullivan Show*; makes his first movie, *Love Me Tender*.

1957—Releases four more number-one songs and two more hit movies, including *Jailhouse Rock*.

1958—Is inducted into U.S. Army; his mother, Gladys, dies; he is shipped out to Germany; his popular movie *King Creole* is released.

1959—Serves successfully in the army; becomes involved romantically with fourteen-year-old Priscilla Beaulieu.

1960—Completes service in the army and returns to United States; releases more hit albums and songs; stars in *GI Blues* and *Flaming Star* movies.

1961–1965—Continues to release strings of albums, singles, and movies, which gradually begin to lose commercial appeal; Priscilla Beaulieu comes to Memphis in 1963 to finish high school and moves into Graceland.

1966—Proposes to Priscilla just before Christmas.

1967—Purchases the Circle G ranch in Mississippi; releases gospel album *How Great Thou Art*, which wins a Grammy Award; marries Priscilla on May 1.

1968—Welcomes birth of daughter, Lisa Marie, on February 1; performs in a television special that relaunches his career.

1969—Films his last theatrical movie, *Change of Habit*; releases "In the Ghetto" and "Suspicious Minds," his two hottest songs in years; the latter becomes his first number-one hit in seven years; performs in wildly successful stage shows in Las Vegas.

1970—Launches first tour since 1957; stars in documentary film *That's the Way It Is*; meets President Richard Nixon.

1971—Continues to tour and perform in Las Vegas; sets attendance records at the Houston Astrodome; receives lifetime achievement award from the National Academy of Recording Arts and Sciences.

1972—Releases gospel album *He Touched Me*, for which he receives his second Grammy; sells out Madison Square Garden for four shows; separates from Priscilla and begins dating Linda Thompson.

1973—Performs in *Aloha from Hawaii*, a special concert beamed live via satellite around the world and viewed by more than a billion people; receives a

Golden Globe for the *Elvis on Tour* documentary filmed a year earlier; signs new recording contract with RCA and new management contract with Colonel Parker; finalizes divorce from Priscilla.

1974–1975—Concert tours and Las Vegas shows continue, but the quality is variable and Elvis's health begins to decline.

1976—Records his last single, "Way Down"; breaks up with Linda Thompson and begins dating Ginger Alden.

1977—Tours early in year but experiences increasing health problems; dies on August 16 just prior to launching another tour.

1979—Vernon Presley dies of a heart attack.

1982—Graceland opens to the public.

1986—Elvis is among the first inductees into the Rock and Roll Hall of Fame.

1992—Elvis's image appears on a postage stamp.

2008—Although he has been dead for more than thirty years, Elvis continues to generate an average of $45 million in annual revenues.

Glossary

amphetamine—A type of drug that stimulates the nervous system.

artifact—An object that relates to a person, time, or place.

aspire—To hope for or plan for.

audition—To try out for.

blatant—Obvious, often in a loud or rude manner.

bloated—Swollen or puffed up.

chronic—Continuing for a long time; having long had a disease or other health problem.

debut—Appearing or doing something for the first time.

deferment—Temporary postponement for entering military service.

demeaning—Degrading, embarrassing.

disquiet—A state of anxiety or uneasiness.

endorsement—A recommendation of something or someone.

entourage—A group of attendants, usually associated with a person of importance.

eviction—To expel, especially as in making someone leave a building, usually through a legal process.

foreshadow—To indicate or suggest something before it happens.

furlough—A vacation or leave of absence from military service.

gyrations—Movements in a circular or spiral motion.

icon—A symbol or image that represents something.

inducted—Admitted as a member, especially into military service.

jailbird A person who has served time in jail.

jaundice—A condition in which the skin is yellowed, usually because of a disease.

mesmerize—To fascinate or hold spellbound.

munitions—Materials used in war, especially weapons and ammunition.

oblivion—The state of being forgotten or unknown.

prophecy—A prediction of the future.

putrid—Of low quality; rotten.

ravishing—Extremely beautiful.

rendition—A version or translation of something.

renowned—Well known, famous.

secluded—Private, sheltered from public activity.

sharecropper—A tenant farmer who pays as rent a share of the crop.

sporadic—Occasional, happening at irregular intervals.

svelte—Slender.

venue—A site or place where an event takes place.

vindicated—Upheld or justified.

Chapter Notes

Chapter 1. Elvis Presley, the King

1. Peter Guralnick, *Last Train to Memphis: The Rise of Elvis Presley* (Boston: Little, Brown, 1994), p. 338.
2. Jennifer Rosenberg, "1956—Elvis Gyrates on Ed Sullivan's Show," *About.com*, n.d., <http://history1900s.about.com/od/1950s/qt/elvissullivan.htm> (June 1, 2009).
3. Glenn C. Altschuler, *All Shook Up: How Rock 'N' Roll Changed America* (New York: Oxford University Press, 2003), pp. 90–91.
4. Fred Bronson, *The Billboard Book of Number 1 Hits* (New York: Billboard Books, 2003), p. 10.
5. Guralnick, p. 311.
6. Adam Victor, *The Elvis Encyclopedia* (New York: Overlook Duckworth, Peter Mayer Publishers, Inc., 2008), p. 370.
7. Jerry Hopkins, *Elvis: The Biography* (London: Plexus, 2007), p. 93.
8. Peter Guralnick and Ernst Jorgensen, *Elvis Day By Day: The Definitive Record of His Life and Music* (New York: Ballantine Books, 1999), p. 95.
9. Rosenberg.
10. Altschuler, p. 91.

Chapter 2. The Twin Who Lived

1. Alanna Nash, *Elvis Aaron Presley: Revelations From the Memphis Mafia* (New York: HarperCollins, 1995), p. 9.
2. Jerry Hopkins, *Elvis: The Biography* (London: Plexus, 2007), p. 21.

3. Peter Guralnick, *Last Train to Memphis: The Rise of Elvis Presley* (Boston: Little, Brown and Company, 1994), p. 13.

4. Paul Simpson, *The Rough Guide to Elvis* (London: Rough Guides Ltd., 2004), p. 8.

5. Gene Smiley, "Great Depression," *Library of Economics and Liberty*, n.d., <http://www.econlib.org/library/Enc/GreatDepression.html> (June 1, 2009).

6. Nash, p. 11.

7. Elaine Dundy, *Elvis and Gladys* (New York: Macmillan, 1985), p. 57.

8. Ibid., p. 58.

9. Nash, p. 13.

10. Guralnick, p. 14.

11. Larry Geller and Joel Spector with Patricia Romanowski, *"If I Can Dream": Elvis' Own Story* (New York: Avon Books, 1989), p. 30.

12. Helen Clutton, *Everything Elvis: Fantastic Facts About the King* (London: Virgin Books Ltd., 2004), p. 75.

13. Simpson, p. 9.

14. Peter Harry Brown and Pat H. Broeske, *Down at the End of Lonely Street: The Life and Death of Elvis Presley* (New York: Dutton, 1997), p. 11.

15. Ibid., p. 11.

16. Simpson, p. 52.

17. Guralnick, p. 16.

18. Dundy, p. 100.

19. Ibid., p. 5.

20. Guralnick, pp. 16–17.

Chapter 3. Making Music

1. Elaine Dundy, *Elvis and Gladys* (New York: Macmillan, 1985), p. 93.

2. Peter Guralnick, *Last Train to Memphis: The Rise of Elvis Presley* (Boston, Little, Brown, 1994), p. 21.

3. Ibid., p. 17.
4. Larry Geller and Joel Spector with Patricia Romanowski, *"If I Can Dream": Elvis' Own Story* (New York: Avon Books, 1989), p. 31.
5. Guralnick, p. 18.
6. Ibid.
7. Paul Simpson, *The Rough Guide to Elvis* (London: Rough Guides Ltd., 2004), p. 11.
8. Dundy, p. 101.
9. Guralnick, p. 19.
10. Dundy, p. 101.
11. Guralnick, p. 19.
12. Ibid., pp. 19–20.
13. Adam Victor, *The Elvis Dictionary* (New York: Overlook Duckworth, Peter Mayer Publishers, Inc., 2008), p. 84.
14. Guralnick, p. 25.
15. Ibid., p. 26.
16. Simpson, p. 14.
17. Dundy, p. 125.
18. Guralnick, p. 28.

Chapter 4. Moving to Memphis

1. Jerry Hopkins, *Elvis: The Biography* (London: Plexus, 2007), p. 28.
2. Alanna Nash with Billy Smith, Marty Lacker, and Lamar Fike, *Elvis Aaron Presley: Revelations from the Memphis Mafia* (New York: HarperCollins, 1995), p. 21.
3. Peter Guralnick, *Last Train to Memphis: The Rise of Elvis Presley* (Boston: Little, Brown, 1994), pp. 32–33.
4. Ibid., p. 33.
5. Peter Guralnick and Ernst Jorgensen, *Elvis Day By Day: The Definitive Record of His Life and Music* (New York: Ballantine Pubishing Group, 1999), p. 7.
6. Guralnick, p. 36.

7. Ibid., p. 35.
8. Paul Simpson, *The Rough Guide to Elvis* (London: Rough Guides Ltd., 2004), p. 419.
9. Elaine Dundy, *Elvis and Gladys* (New York: Macmillan, 1985), p. 139.
10. Hopkins, p. 36.
11. Guralnick, p. 45.
12. Ibid., pp. 46–47.
13. Dundy, p. 153.
14. Guralnick and Jorgensen, p. 12.

Chapter 5. Breaking Through

1. "What Things Cost: Prices for 1954," *The Fifties Web*, n.d., <http://www.fiftiesweb.com/pop/prices-1954.htm> (June 12, 2009).
2. Jerry Hopkins, *Elvis: The Biography* (London: Plexus Publishing Limited, 2007), p. 40.
3. Helen Clutton, *Everything Elvis: Fantastic Facts About the King* (London: Virgin Books Ltd., 2004), p. 6.
4. Pamela Clarke Keogh, *Elvis Presley: The Man. The Life. The Legend* (New York: Atria Books, 2004), p. 23.
5. Adam Victor, *The Elvis Encyclopedia* (New York: Overlook Duckworth, Peter Mayer Publishers, Inc., 2008), p. 308.
6. Peter Guralnick, *Last Train to Memphis: The Rise of Elvis Presley* (New York: Little, Brown, 1994), p. 80.
7. Victor, p. 48.
8. Elaine Dundy, *Elvis and Gladys* (New York: Macmillan, 1985), p. 176.
9. Paul Simpson, *The Rough Guide to Elvis* (London: Rough Guides Ltd., 2004), p. 18.
10. Glenn C. Altschuler, *All Shook Up: How Rock 'N' Roll Changed America* (New York: Oxford University Press, 2003), p. 27.
11. Dundy, p. 179.

12. Peter Guralnick and Ernst Jorgensen, *Elvis Day By Day: The Definitive Record of His Life and Music* (New York: Ballantine Publishing Group, 1999), p. 19.

13. Robert Sullivan, ed., *Remembering Elvis 30 Years Later* (New York: Life Books, 2007), p. 18.

14. Guralnick and Jorgensen, p. 19.

15. Guralnick, p. 115.

16. Ibid.

17. Ibid., pp. 129–130.

18. Guralnick and Jorgenson, p. 26.

19. Ibid.

20. Guralnick, p. 156.

Chapter 6. Ascending the Throne

1. Peter Guralnick and Ernst Jorgensen, *Elvis Day By Day: The Definitive Record of His Life and Music* (New York: Ballantine Books, 1999), p. 27.

2. Jerry Hopkins, *Elvis: The Biography* (London: Plexus Publishing, 2007), p. 57.

3. Alanna Nash, *The Colonel: The Extraordinary Story of Colonel Tom Parker and Elvis Presley* (Chicago: Chicago Review Press, 2004), p. 119.

4. Peter Guralnick, *Last Train to Memphis: The Rise of Elvis Presley* (Boston: Little, Brown, 1994), p. 181.

5. Ibid., p. 185.

6. Hopkins, p. 69.

7. Ibid., p. 74.

8. Toby Creswell, *1001 Songs: The Great Songs of All Time* (New York: Thunder's Mouth Press, 2006), p. 380.

9. Guralnick, p. 233.

10. Guralnick and Jorgensen, p. 54.

11. Ibid., p. 53.

12. Hopkins, p. 84.

13. Ibid., p. 81.

14. Glenn C. Altschuler, *All Shook Up: How Rock 'n' Roll Changed America* (New York: Oxford University Press, 2003), p. 89.

15. Adam Victor, *The Elvis Encyclopedia* (New York: Overlook Duckworth, Peter Mayer Publishers, 2008), p. 370.

16. Guralnick, pp. 285–286.

17. Helen Clutton, *Everything Elvis: Fantastic Facts About the King* (London: Virgin Books Ltd., 2004), p. 16.

18. Loanne M. Parker, "Colonel Tom Parker," *Rockabilly Hall of Fame*, n.d., <http://www.rockabillyhall.com/ColTom.html> (June 14, 2009).

19. Nash, p. 119.

20. Victor, p. 370.

Chapter 7. The King Reigns

1. Adam Victor, *The Elvis Encyclopedia* (New York: Overlook Duckworth, Peter Mayer Publishers, 2008), p. 318.

2. Jerry Hopkins, *Elvis: The Biography* (London: Plexus Publishing, 2007), p. 122.

3. Victor, p. 269.

4. "National Average Wage Index," *Social Security Online,* October 16, 2008, <http://www.ssa.gov/OACT/COLA/AWI.html> (February 6, 2009).

5. Elaine Dundy, *Elvis and Gladys* (New York: Macmillan, 1985), p. 293.

6. Peter Guralnick, *Last Train to Memphis: The Rise of Elvis Presley* (Boston: Little, Brown, 1994), p. 417.

7. Paul Simpson, *The Rough Guide to Elvis* (London: Rough Guides Ltd., 2004), p. 27.

8. Robert Palmer, *Rock & Roll: An Unruly History* (New York: Harmony Books, 1995), p. 51.

9. Hopkins, p. 126.

10. Chris Talbott, "Elvis Fan Club's License Plate Is Fit for a 'King'," *Elvis Australia,* n.d., <http:// www.elvis.com.au/presley/news/elvis_fan_clubs_license _plate_is_fit_for_a_king.shtml> (June 15, 2009).

11. Hopkins, p. 125.

12. Guralnick, p. 440.

13. Ibid., p. 441.

14. Dundy, p. 294.

15. Ibid., p. 294.

16. Robert Sullivan, ed., *Remembering Elvis: 30 Years Later* (New York: Life Books, 2007), p. 70.

17. Alanna Nash, *The Colonel: The Extraordinary Story of Colonel Tom Parker and Elvis Presley* (Chicago: Chicago Review Press, 2003), p. 175.

18. Hopkins, p. 128.

19. Ibid.

20. Simpson, p. 315.

Chapter 8. In the Army

1. Elaine Dundy, *Elvis and Gladys* (New York: Macmillan, 1985), p. 319.

2. Jerry Hopkins, *Elvis: The Biography* (London: Plexus, 2007), pp. 134–135.

3. Ibid., p. 135.

4. "Elvis Presley Graceland + Army Induction," *Elvis Presley Music,* n.d., <http://www.elvispresleymusic .com.au/pictures/1958_march_24.html> (February 26, 2009).

5. Alanna Nash with Billy Smith, Marty Lacker, and Lamar Fike, *Elvis Aaron Presley: Revelations from the Memphis Mafia* (New York: HarperCollins, 1995), p. 131.

6. Marie Clayton, *Elvis: The Illustrated Biography* (Croxley Green, U.K.: Transatlantic Press, 2008), p. 87.

7. Larry Geller and Joel Spector with Patricia Romanowski, *"If I Can Dream": Elvis' Own Story* (New York: Avon, 1989), p. 38.
8. Robert Sullivan, ed., *Remembering Elvis: 30 Years Later* (New York: Life Books, 2007), p. 80.
9. Peter Guralnick and Ernst Jorgensen, *Elvis Day By Day: The Definitive Record of His Life and Music* (New York: Ballantine Books, 1999), p. 126.
10. Andreas Schroer, *Private Presley* (New York: William and Morrow, 1993), p. 49.
11. Ibid., p. 140.
12. Nash with Smith, Lacker, and Fike, p. 147.
13. Hopkins, p. 149.
14. Schroer, p. 54.
15. Peter Guralnick, *Careless Love: The Unmaking of Elvis Presley* (Boston: Little, Brown and Company, 1999), p. 41.
16. Hopkins, p. 153.
17. Schroer, p. 153.
18. Sullivan, p. 87.

Chapter 9. Back on Top, But for How Long?

1. Robert Sullivan, ed., *Remembering Elvis: 30 Years Later* (New York: Life Books, 2007), p. 90.
2. Paul Simpson, *The Rough Guide to Elvis* (London: Rough Guides Ltd., 2004), pp. 305–306.
3. Pauline Kael, *"This Is Elvis,"* The Niuean Pop Cultural Archive, n.d., <http://www.unknown.nu/misc/elvis.html> (February 28, 2009).
4. John Robertson, *Elvis Presley: The Complete Guide to His Music* (London: Omnibus Books, 2004), p. 34.
5. Jerry Hopkins, *Elvis: The Biography* (London: Plexus, 2007), p. 159.

6. Robertson, p. 49.
7. Ibid., p. 50.
8. Bob Spitz, *The Beatles: The Biography* (New York: Little, Brown, and Company, 2005), p. 582.
9. Helen Clutton, *Everything Elvis: Fantastic Facts About the King* (London: Virgin Books Ltd., 2004), p. 70.
10. Peter Guralnick, *Careless Love: The Unmaking of Elvis Presley* (Boston: Little, Brown and Company, 1999), p. 68.
11. Peter Harry Brown and Pat H. Broeske, *Down at the End of Lonely Street: The Life and Death of Elvis Presley* (New York: Dutton, 1997), p. 237.
12. Adam Victor, *The Elvis Encyclopedia* (New York: Overlook Duckworth, Peter Mayer Publishers, 2008), p. 467.
13. Guralnick, p. 87.
14. Larry Geller and Joel Spector with Patricia Romanowski, *"If I Can Dream": Elvis' Own Story* (New York: Avon Books, 1989), p. 23.
15. David Ritz, ed., *Elvis by the Presleys* (New York: Crown, 2005), p. 111.
16. Brown and Broeske, p. 292.

Chapter 10. Marriage, Birth, and Rebirth

1. Priscilla Presley, *Elvis and Me* (New York: G.P. Putnam's Sons, 1985), p. 222.
2. Ibid., p. 216.
3. Peter Guralnick, *Careless Love: The Unmaking of Elvis Presley* (Boston: Little, Brown and Company, 1999), p. 249.
4. Joe Moscheo, *The Gospel Side of Elvis* (New York: Center Street, 2007), p. 58.

5. Alanna Nash with Billy Smith, Marty Lacker, and Lamar Fike, *Elvis Aaron Presley: Revelations from the Memphis Mafia* (New York: HarperCollins, 1995), p. 432.

6. Jerry Hopkins, *Elvis: The Biography* (London: Plexus Publishing, 2007), p. 199.

7. David Ritz, ed., *Elvis by the Presleys* (New York: Crown, 2005), p. 130.

8. Presley, p. 231.

9. Peter Harry Brown and Pat H. Broeske, *Down at the End of Lonely Street: The Life and Death of Elvis Presley* (New York: Dutton, 1997), p. 310.

10. Peter Guralnick and Ernst Jorgensen, *Elvis Day By Day: The Definitive Record of His Life and Music* (New York: Ballantine Books, 1999), p. 232.

11. Paul Simpson, *The Rough Guide to Elvis* (London: Rough Guides Ltd., 2004), p. 358.

12. Robert Sullivan, ed., *Remembering Elvis: 30 Years Later* (New York: Life Books, 2007), p. 109.

13. "Elvis Presley—If I Can Dream," *YouTube*, <http://www.youtube.com/watch?v=mfvsepvgCCc& feature=PlayList&p=C391FC681B2C64F4&playnext =1&playnext_from=PL&index=17>

14. Simpson, p. 118.

15. Toby Creswell, *1001 Songs: The Great Songs of All Time* (New York: Thunder Mouth's Press, 2006), p. 453.

16. John Robertson, *Elvis Presley: The Complete Guide to His Music* (London: Omnibus Books, 2004), p. 64.

17. Anthony DeCurtis and James Henke, eds., with Holly George-Warren, *The Rolling Stone Album Guide* (New York: Random House, 1992), p. 556.

18. Guralnick, p. 337.

19. Guralnick and Jorgensen, p. 259.

20. Hopkins, p. 227.

Chapter 11. Caught in a Trap

1. Jerry Hopkins, *Elvis: The Biography* (London: Plexus Publishing, 2007), p. 232.

2. Peter Guralnick and Ernst Jorgensen, *Elvis Day By Day: The Definitive Record of His Life and Music* (New York: Ballantine Books, 1999), p. 269.

3. Priscilla Presley, *Elvis and Me* (New York: G.P. Putnam's Sons, 1985), p. 277.

4. Marie Clayton, *Elvis: The Illustrated Biography* (Croxley Green, U.K.: Transatlantic Press, 2008), p. 179.

5. Adam Victor, *The Elvis Encyclopedia* (New York: Overlook Duckworth, Peter Mayer Publishers, Inc., 2008), p. 405.

6. Presley, p. 300.

7. Paul Simpson, *The Rough Guide to Elvis* (London: Rough Guides Ltd., 2004), p. 47.

8. Peter Harry Brown and Pat H. Broeske, *Down at the End of Lonely Street: The Life and Death of Elvis Presley* (New York: Dutton, 1997), p. 361.

9. Simpson, pp. 285–286.

10. John Robertson, *Elvis Presley: The Complete Guide to His Music* (New York: Omnibus Press, 2004), p. 69.

11. Simpson, p. 372.

12. Hopkins, p. 306.

13. David Ritz, ed., *Elvis by the Presleys* (New York: Crown, 2005), p. 163.

14. Robert Sullivan, ed., *Remembering Elvis: 30 Years Later* (New York: Life Books, 2007), p. 112.

15. Guralnick and Jorgensen, p. 351.

16. Brown and Broeske, p. 362.

Chapter 12. The King Is Dead

1. Peter Guralnick and Ernst Jorgensen, *Elvis Day By Day: The Definitive Record of His Life and Music* (New York: Ballantine Books, 1999), p. 370.
2. Paul Simpson, *The Rough Guide to Elvis* (London: Rough Guides Ltd., 2004), p. 57.
3. Peter Guralnick, *Careless Love: The Unmaking of Elvis Presley* (Boston: Little, Brown and Company, 1999), p. 628.
4. Guralnick and Jorgensen, p. 372.
5. Jerry Hopkins, *Elvis: The Biography* (London: Plexus Publishing, 2007), p. 367.
6. Ibid., p. 368.
7. Guralnick, p. 638.
8. Hopkins, p. 376.
9. Ibid., p. 380.
10. Guralnick and Jorgensen, p. 379.
11. Guralnick, p. 649.
12. Ibid., p. 649.
13. *Elvis Presley News.com*, n.d., <http://www.elvispresleynews.com/ElvisFuneral.html> (June 15, 2009).
14. Hopkins, p. 385.

Chapter 13. Long Live the King

1. "Top 10 Richest Dead Celebrities," *SnagWireMedia.com*, n.d., <http://snagwiremedia.com/top-10-richest-dead-celebrities/> (June 15, 2009).
2. Jerry Hopkins, *Elvis: The Biography* (London: Plexus Publishing Ltd., 2007), p. 391.
3. Adam Victor, *The Elvis Encyclopedia* (New York: Overlook Duckworth, Peter Mayer Publishers, 2008), p. 393.
4. Hopkins, p. 392.

5. Victor, p. 208.
6. *Elvis Presley's Graceland: The Official Guidebook* (Memphis: Elvis Presley Enterprises Inc., 1993), p. 26.
7. Alanna Nash, "Welcome to Graceland," *American Profile.com*, n.d., <http://www.americanprofile.com/article/28656.html?printable=true> (June 15, 2009).
8. "Biography," *Lisa Marie Presley Online*, n.d., <http://www.lisamarieonline.net/lisa/bio.php> (June 15, 2009).
9. Associated Press, "Presley Opens up About Marriage to Jackson," *MSNBC.com*, n.d., <http://www.msnbc.msn.com/id/7330946/> (June 15, 2009).
10. Amy Elisa Keith, "Photo Exclusive: Lisa Marie Presley's Twin Baby Girls," *People.com*, n.d., <http://www.people.com/people/article/0,,20252307,00.html> (June 15, 2009).
11. Victor, p. 157.
12. "Livewire's top 10: Who Made Who? The Top Ten Most Influential Rock Artists of All-Time," *Livewire.com*, n.d., <http://www.concertlivewire.com/top10in.htm> (June 20, 2009).
13. Glenn C. Altschuler, *All Shook Up: How Rock 'N' Roll Changed America* (New York: Oxford University Press, 2003), p. 189.
14. Bob Spitz, *The Beatles* (New York: Little, Brown, 2005), p. 41.
15. Fred Bronson, *The Billboard Book of Number One Hits* (New York: Billboard Books, 2003), p. 10.
16. Toby Creswell, *1001 Songs: The Great Songs of All Time* (New York: Thunder's Mouth Press, 2006), pp. 46–47.

Further Reading

Books

Denenberg, Barry. *All Shook Up!: The Life and Death of Elvis Presley*. New York: Scholastic Press, 2001.

Gogerly, Liz. *Elvis Presley: The King of Rock and Roll*. Chicago: Raintree, 2004.

Hampton, Wilborn. *Elvis Presley: A Twentieth Century Life*. New York: Viking, 2007.

Klein, George. *Elvis Presley: The Family Album*. New York: Little, Brown and Co., 2007.

Rosen, Steven. *History of Rock*. St. Catharines, Ont.: Crabtree Pub., 2009.

Internet Addresses

Elvis Presley Official Web site
  <http://www.elvis.com>

Elvis News
  <http://www.elvisnews.com>

Index